Worthington Chauncey Ford, Jonathan Boucher

Letters of Jonathan Boucher to George Washington

Worthington Chauncey Ford, Jonathan Boucher

Letters of Jonathan Boucher to George Washington

ISBN/EAN: 9783337016203

Printed in Europe, USA, Canada, Australia, Japan

Cover: Foto ©ninafisch / pixelio.de

More available books at **www.hansebooks.com**

ASHINGTON-BOUCHER CORRESPONDENCE.

W. I. Newman Pinx.

J. Condé sculp

JONATHAN BOUCHER, M.A.

LETTERS

OF

JONATHAN BOUCHER

TO

GEORGE WASHINGTON.

COLLECTED AND EDITED

BY

WORTHINGTON CHAUNCEY FORD.

BROOKLYN, N. Y.:
HISTORICAL PRINTING CLUB.
1899.

D. CLAPP & SON, Printers,
BOSTON.

LETTERS OF JONATHAN BOUCHER TO GEORGE WASHINGTON.

THE following letters possess more than a personal interest. It was an accidental circumstance, a connection with Washington, that lent some notoriety to Jonathan Boucher. It is his ideas on education that makes these records of permanent interest, for they throw some light upon the conceptions of education entertained nearly a century and a half ago in Virginia.

Boucher, tutor, divine and lexicographer, was born at Blencogo, a small hamlet in the parish of Bromfield, England, 12 March, 1738. He received some schooling at Wigton, and towards the end of the year 1755, went to Workington, in order to study mathematics, under Rev. Mr. Ritson, who, Boucher states in his autobiography, of which only extracts have been printed, "was a character, and thought so even in a part of the world that is fruitful in characters." He must have excelled in mathematics, for as schoolmaster at Workington and minister of a chapel at Clifton, he received £40 a year. Yet by taking private pupils he "not only brought up his family, but saved a thousand pounds."

With him Boucher remained four years. What happened then may best be described in his own words.

" Early in 1759, Mr. James heard that Mr. Younger, a respectable merchant in Whitehaven, wanted a young man to go out as private tutor to a gentleman's sons in Virginia . . . . I was to enter into pay on the day of my leaving England ; to have my passage gratis ; to have my board and sixty pounds sterling a year for teaching four boys, with liberty to take four more, on such terms as I could agree for, on my arrival . . . . On the 12th of July I landed safe at Urbanna, near the mouth of Rappahannock river ; and soon after got to the place of my destination, viz., Captain Dixon's, at Port Royal, on the same river, and met with a cordial reception.* . . . .

Being hospitable as well as wealthy, Captain Dixon's house was much resorted to, but chiefly by toddy-drinking company. Port Royal was inhabited in a great measure by factors from Scotland and their dependents; and the circumjacent country by planters, in general in middling circumstances. There was not a literary man, for aught I could find, nearer than in the country I had just left; nor were literary attainments, beyond merely reading or writing, at all in vogue or repute. In such society it was little

---

* Mr. R. A. Brock, lately librarian of the Virginia Historical Society, tells me that this was doubtless Roger Dixon, who died just before the Revolution. " He was a vestryman of St. George's Parish, Spotsylvania Co., in 1768, and a little later appears to have had pecuniary reverses. In 1770, Thomas Nelson, Jr., had a claim for a considerable amount due British merchants to collect from him."

likely I should add to my own little stock of learning; in fact, there were no longer any inducements . . . . In all the two years I lived at Port Royal I did not form a single friendship on which I can now look back with much approbation, though I had a numerous acquaintance and many intimacies . . . .

I was now once more quite to seek, and as much at a loss as ever as to a profession for life. My thoughts had long been withdrawn from the church. Yet happily, a train of unforeseen circumstances now led me back to this my original bias, and at last made me an ecclesiastic.

A Mr. Giberne* was rector of Hanover parish, in King George's County, and lived across the river, directly opposite to Port Royal . . . . He was now engaged to marry a rich widow in Richmond County, and the parish there being vacant, and offered to him, it was natural he should accept it. All at once, and without the least solicitation on my part, or even thinking about it, that which he was about to leave was offered to me. The suddenness of the thing and my deep sense of their kindness, rather than my not knowing what else to do with myself, determined me to accept of it. I did so, and was to sail for England for Orders the week after . . . . Captain Stanley, of the Christian, promised to give me a passage home and back again gratis. I embarked on board the Christian about the middle of December, and about the middle of the following month in 1762, I arrived in Whitehaven, after a rough and tempestuous passage . . . .

All the little time I now staid in England was one continued scene of bustle and hurry. I went from Whitehaven to London for Ordination, and Bishop Osbaldeston being then just come to that see, I was long detained and much plagued before I succeeded . . . .

It was a remarkable coincidence, though perfectly accidental, that I again landed on the 12th of July, and again at Urianna . . . .

An incident now occurred, apparently of no moment, but which, as it led to some circumstances of great moment in my little history, I must set down. One Sunday, as I was riding to my church at Leeds, on the road I fell in and joined company with a stranger gentleman. He was from Maryland, of the name of Swift, distantly related to the family of the celebrated Dean; and being a merchant, his errand in my neighbourhood was to secure a large debt owing to him which he thought, and not without reason, to be somewhat hazardous. I was happy enough to point out to him a way of effecting his purposes, which might not have occurred to himself, but which happily succeeded. On his return he spoke of my kind offices and myself with such warmth that next spring four of his most respectable neighbours sent four boys under my care, and thus began my acquaintance in Maryland . . . .

I seemed now to be somewhat in a flourishing way, and as I was very diligent and faithful in my employment, my character was soon established. But behold, early in August I was seized with a violent fever, from which it was thought little less than miraculous that I ever recovered. It was late in November before I was able to stir out of my own doors . . . . During

---

* Of this "Rev." Isaac William Giberne the commissary wrote in 1766: "His mother is a milliner in the city of Westminster. He was not bred to the church, but was sometime a clerk in some office on Tower Hill. He obtained orders and came here under the countenance and protection of the present governor [Fauquier]. He purchased the disgust of the Clergy at his first coming by unsuccessful endeavors to reconcile them to an Act of which they had sent a complaint to England, boldly setting his Youth and Rawness in opposition to the past and present feelings of long experience. . . . Many of the Laity think him too fond of cards and gaming for one of his cloth. He has removed from one Parish to another two or three times." A characteristic letter of his is printed in my *Letters of William Lee*, I. 70.

this illness my countryman and acquaintance, the Rev. Mr. Dawson, of St. Mary's, in Carolina County, had died. Port Royal, where I had formerly lived, was in this parish; and my friends so earnestly solicited me to succeed him, that, after some hesitation, I at length consented, but not before the people of Hanover, who had so generously chosen me for their minister under many disadvantages, also gave me their entire approbation. They went so far as to continue my salary a quarter of a year after I left them; an instance of generosity which I hope never to forget . . . . St. Mary's was not a pleasant place, neither had it good water; but there was a good house, and another old one, which at a little expense might be made such an one as I wanted. To this place I removed early in the spring. And now, besides adding largely to the furniture of the house, I bought stocks of cattle, and horses, and slaves.

But my industry and exertions were extraordinary. I had the care of a large parish, and my church was eleven miles distance from me; neither had I yet any stock of sermons. My first overseer turned out good for nothing, and I soon parted with him, so that all the care of the plantation devolved on me; and though it was my first attempt in that way, I made a good crop. I had now also increased my number of boys to nearly thirty, most of them the sons of persons of the first condition in the colony. They all boarded with me, and I wholly superintended them myself, without any usher, for two years.

At this glebe of St. Mary's I lived, I believe, seven years. I had a good neighbourhood, and many hospitable and friendly neighbours; and I had a great turn for plantation improvements, which I indulged to a great extent. Yet upon the whole I cannot look back on this period of my life with much satisfaction. It was busy and bustling, but it was not pleasant, inasmuch as it was very little such a course of life as a literary man should wish to lead. And though it was neither wholly unprofitable to myself, nor, I trust, wholly useless to others, yet I attained neither of these purposes to such a degree as I now think I might have done. . . . .

He followed Ritson's example and took pupils, two of whom, young Custis, and a Mr. Carr who afterward married a sister of Boucher's wife, went with him to Maryland. It is in regard to Custis that these letters were written, but before introducing them a few more sentences may be taken from the autobiography, descriptive of the intellectual condition of the colony.

On my removal to Annapolis the scene was once more almost quite new to me. It was then the genteelest town in North America, and many of its inhabitants were highly respectable as to station, fortune, and education. I hardly know a town in England so desirable to live in as Annapolis then was. It was the seat of government, and the residence of the Governor and all the great officers of state, as well as of the most eminent lawyers, physicians, and families of opulence and note. . . . .

A very handsome theatre was built whilst I stayed there by subscription; and as the church was old and ordinary, and this theatre was built on land belonging to the church, I drew up a petition in verse in behalf of the old church, which was inserted in the Gazette, and did me credit. And this I think was one of the first things that made me to be taken notice of. I also wrote some verses on one of the actresses, and a prologue or two. And thus, as I was now once more among literary men, my attention was once more drawn to literary pursuits, and I became of some note as a writer. The Rector of Annapolis is officially chaplain to the Lower House; and the salary was but about 10*l* currency a session, and even that ill-paid. It seemed an indignity to offer or to receive a salary beneath that of the door-keeper or mace-bearer; and so I wrote a letter to the assembly in as handsome terms as I could, that I would, if they so pleased, serve them for nothing, but that, if I was paid at all, I would be paid as a gentleman. This transaction also made much talk in the country, gaining me some friends and more enemies.

Three or four social and literary men proposed the institution of a weekly club under the title of the Homony Club, of which I was the first president. It was, in fact, the best club in all respects I have ever heard of, as the sole object of it was to promote innocent mirth and ingenious humour. We had a secretary, and books in which all our proceedings were recorded,* and as every member conceived himself bound to contribute some composition, either in verse or prose, and we had also many mirthfully ingenious debates, our archives soon swelled to two or three folios, replete with much miscellaneous wit and fun. I had a great share in its proceedings; and it soon grew into such fame that the governor and all the principal people of the country ambitiously solicited the honour of being members or honorary visitants. It lasted as long as I stayed in Annapolis, and was finally broken up only when the troubles began and put an end to everything that was pleasant and proper. . . . .

At the outbreak of the Revolution Boucher remained loyal to the king, and was obliged to leave Maryland. Going to England he received a pension from the crown, and devoted himself to philology. He died in 1804.

It must be admitted that Boucher was, in ability, much above the ordinary divine to be found in Virginia at that time. Many very peculiar characters were exported from England to lead the souls of the American colonists into the paths of righteousness. If we were to judge the sincerity of the church by the character of some of its exponents and agents to be found in Virginia, the result would be discouraging. Like the merchandise sent to America, many of the clergymen might have been called "colonials," meaning a quality of article not good enough to be used at home, but quite good enough for use in a colony thousands of miles away, and where the curing of tobacco was of equal importance with curing of souls. No scandal ever attached to Boucher. He owned and worked slaves, but that has a necessary incident where free labor could not exist owing to the prevalence of slavery. He taught his slaves, and even made some of them schoolmasters for the rest. He was a Tory, but a good part of the wealth and intelligence of the colonies remained loyal. He loved horse racing, but against that may be set his ardent desire for intellectual fellowship, and the Homony Club, one of the earliest literary clubs in America.

Wherever Washington's letters throw light upon those of Boucher

* One or more of these volumes may be seen in the collection of the Pennsylvania Historical Society.

I have used them. A letter from the President of King's College (now Columbia University) is inserted as germane to the subject. In every case the letters are printed as the writers wrote them, as any revision of text would destroy one of the main reasons for printing — the illustration of character in the writer.

Boucher to Washington. *

CAROLINE, 13 June, 1768.

Sir,

I think myself much obliged to you for the flattering Preference given me. in thinking me a proper person to undertake the Direction of mast^r Custis's Education. And I will not hesitate to confess to you, that it wou'd mortify me not a little to be depriv'd of so acceptable an Opportunity of obtaining some Credit to myself; which I flatter myself there wou'd be no Danger of, from so promising a youth. Yet am I under a necessity of informing you of a Circumstance in my affairs, which may probably lead you to look out for another Tutor for your Ward. Preferments in the church in Virginia are so extremely scanty, that I have for some time been endeavouring to establish an interest in Maryland, where, I doubt not but you know, the Livings are much better. I happened to be in Annapolis. chiefly upon this Business, at the Time your Letter reach'd this Place: and tho' I have already met with two Disappointments. yet I have rec^d. fresh Promises that I shall now soon be provided for. If This happen at all, as I have all ye Reason in ye world to believe that it will. the Parish I expect is That of Annap^s., where also I propose to continue superintending the Education of a few Boys.

Now, Sir, it will be necessary for you to consider, whether in Case such a change sh^d. take Place, it w^d. be agreeable to you that Mast^r. Custis shou'd accompany me thither: for, otherwise, I can hardly suppose you will think it worth his while to come down hither. probably. for a few months only. For my Part I cannot help imagining that you will think Annap^s. a more eligible situation, as it is. I believe, rather more convenient to you, & a post Town from whence you might have Letters, if necessary. every Week to Alexandria. But This is a matter on which you alone ought to judge. & in which perhaps it becomes not me to give my Opinion. All I have to add is that sh^d. you resolve, at all Events, to trust the young Gentleman to my Care. either Here or in Maryland, I will exert my best Endeavours to render Him worthy of Yours, & his Family's Expectations. And as He is now. as you justly observe, losing Time. wou'd it be amiss to send Him down immediately, if it were only upon Tryal, as I presume He has never yet been remov'd from under the wing of his Parents: You will then, from his own Reports of me & my management of my Pupils. be better able to judge of the Propriety of continuing Him with me. And tho' it be usual

* On May 30, 1768, Washington wrote to Boucher asking if he would be willing to take Master Custis as a pupil. "He is a boy of good genius, about 14 years of age, untainted in his morals & of innocent manners. Two years and upwards he has been reading of Virgil & was (at the time Mr. Macgowan left him) entered upon the Greek Testament." Custis was to have a boy and two horses, and provender for the latter. "If it is necessary for him to provide a Bed, could one be purchased in your neighbourhood? It would save a long carriage." Washington wrote. "I will cheerfully pay Ten or Twelve pounds a year, extraordinary, to engage your peculiar care of, & a watchful eye to him, as he is a promising boy, the last of his family, & will possess a very large Fortune, add to this my anxiety to make him fit for more useful purposes than Horse Racer." The whole letter is in my Writings of Washington, II. 267.

for Boys to find their own Beds, in this case, that wou'd be unnecessary. I will furnish Him for the little Time He will have to stay before I know what my Destiny is to be. As to Terms, &c., These may be settled hereafter. All I shall now say of Them is, that from what I have heard of Coll⁰. Washington's character, they are such as I am well convinced He will not think unreasonable.

I have been under much concern that it was not sooner in my Power to acknowledge the rec^t. of y^r. obliging Letter: this is forwarded by a serv^t. of Mr. Addison's, whom I have requested to send it over to Alexandria, by w^h. Means I hope you will receive it sooner than by Post.

I am, very respectfully, Sir,
Y^r most Obedient &
most Hble Servt.

JONA^n. BOUCHER.

Boucher to Washington.

CAROLINE, 16 June, 1768.

Sir,

Altho' I have already return'd an Ans^r to y^r obliging Letter of the 30th ult: by a serv^t of the Revd Mr Addison's who went from hence a Day or two ago, yet as you seem'd desirous to hear from me as soon as possible, & as Coll⁰ Lewis now informs me that He can furnish me wth an Opp^{ly} directly to your House, I am desirous to convince you, that I have not been inattentive to the Matter of y^r Request. In my former L^r, I have inform'd you of my Expectations of removing shortly to Annap^s, where I propose also to continue to take Care of a few Boys, & have left it to y^{r}self to judge whether, in that Case, it wou'd be agreeable to you & Mrs. Washington, that Mast^r Curtis sh^d accompany me thither, as, unless he shou'd, I imagin'd you wou'd hardly think it worth while to send Him abroad to a school, w^h may probably be broke up in a very few Months. I added also, that sh^d you approve of this, I shou'd be glad He might come down hither, in the Manner you have propos'd, immediately; which, I suppose, He may easily do, as there will be no Occasion for his making much Preparation; since, if I sh^d be so unfortunate as to be again disappointed in Maryland, & be obliged to remain still where I now am, it will be as Easy for you hereafter to furnish Him wth any thing He may happen to want; and in the mean Time, it will be no Inconvenience to me to let Him use one of my Beds, &c. And This is all, or nearly all, I yet have it in my Power to give you for Ans^r: I sincerely wish the Uncertainty of my present Prospects wou'd allow me to speak more positively.

Ever since I have heard of Mast^r Custis, I have wish'd to call Him one of my little Flock; and I am not asham'd to confess to you that, since the Rec^t of y^r Letter, I have wish'd it much more. Engag'd as I have now been for upwards of seven Years in the Education of Youth, you will own it must be mortifying to me to reflect, that I cannot boast of having had the Hou^r to bring up one Scholar. I have had, 'tis true, Youths, whose Fortunes, Inclinations & Capacities all gave me Room for ye most pleasing Hopes: yet I know not how it is, no sooner do They arrive at that Period of Life when They might be expected more successfully to apply to their Studies, than They either marry, or are remov'd from School on some, perhaps even still, less justifiable Motive. You, Sir, however, seem so justly sensible of ye vast Importance of a good Educa^n, that I cannot doubt of your heartily concurring in every Plan that might be propos'd for y° Advantage of y^r Ward: And what I am more particularly pleased with is, the ardent Desire you express for y° Cultiva^n of his moral, as well as his Intellectual Powers. I mean, that He may be made a Good, as well as a learned & sensible Man. That Mast^r Custis may be both is the sincere wish of, *

Sir,

Y^r most obed^t &

most Hble Servt

JONA^n BOUCHER.

Boucher to Washington.

CAROLINE, 15 July, 1768.

Dear Sir,

I have just Time to put a Cover over The Enclosed & to add to the Informa^ns I suppose Mast^r Custis himself has given you, that He has enjoy'd perfect Health ever since you left Him, except^s two or three Days that He complained of a Pain in his stomach, which I at first took for the Cholic, but since think it more likely that it might be owing to Worms. As it easily went off by two or three Medicines I gave Him, and as He has had no Returns, I did not think it necessary to consult Dr. Mercer;† which however, I shall immediately do, if you desire it.

You will oblige us by looking into y^r Books for a Work of Cicero's, De officiis, or his Familiar Epistles — & Livy: & sending Them down by y° first opportunity that [offers].

Be so obliging to me as to excuse the Shortness of this Letter; it shall not be long, ere I will write to you more fully. The Messenger, who is to carry This to y° office, now waits for me.

I am, very respectfully

y^r most obed^t Hble Servt

JONA^n BOUCHER.

Sir,

ST. MARY's, 2 August, 1768.

I do not recollect that Mast^r. Custis has had any Return of y° Pain in his stomach, which I told you I suspected to be occasioned by worms: but as it is but too probable that He may have a little of the ague & Fever in This or y° next month, this complaint, it is not unlikely, may return; and if it does, in any considerable Degree, D^r. Mercer shall be consulted.

Mast^r. Custis is a Boy of so exceedingly mild & meek a Temper, that I meant no more by my Fears, than a Doubt that possibly He might be made uneasy by y° rougher manners of some of his schoolfellows. I am pleas'd, however, to find that He seems to be perfectly easy & happy in his new situation; and as the first shock is now over, I doubt not but He will continue so. You know how much the quest^n. has been agitated between y° advantages of a private & a public Educa^n.: & this young G—man has afforded me occasion to reflect upon it rather more than I had done before. His Educa^n. hitherto may be call'd a private one; & to This, perhaps chiefly, He owes that peculiar Innocence & *sanctity of manners* w^h. are so amiable in Him: but then, is He not, think you, more artless, more unskill'd in a necessary address, than He ought to be, ere He is turn'd out into a world like this? In a private Seminary, his Passions cou'd be seldom arouzed: He had few or no Competitors; and therefore cou'd not so advantageously,

* "June 30, 1768. Went to Mr. Boucher's, dined there, and left Jackey Custis. Returned to Fredericksburg in the afternoon."—*Entry in Washington's Diary.*

† Hugh Mercer, of revolutionary memory.

as in a more pubilc Place, be inured to combat those little oppositions & collisions of Interest, w^h. resemble in miniature the contests y^t happeu in ye gr^t school of ye world. And let our Circumstances in ye world be what They will, yet, considering the thousand unavoidable Troubles that human nature is Heir to, This is a Part of Educaⁿ. tho seldom attended to, w^h. I think of more Importance than almost all ye Rest. When children are taught betimes to bear misfortunes & cross accidents wth becom^s. Fortitude, one half of ye Evils of Life, wth w^h. others are dejected, afflict not Them. Educaⁿ is too generally considered merely as ye acquisⁿ. of knowledge, & ye cultivaⁿ. of ye intellectual Powers. And, agreeably to this notion, wⁿ. we speak of a man well-educated, we seldom mean more than that He has been well instructed in those Languages w^h. are ye avenues to knowledge. But, surely, This is but a partial & imperfect acc^t. of it: & ye aim of Educaⁿ. sh^d be not only to form wise but good men, not only to cultivate ye understanding, but to expand ye Heart, to meliorate ye Temper, & *fix ye gen'rous Purpose in ye glowing Breast.* But whether This can best be done in a private or public school, is a Poiut, on w^h. so much may be said ou both sides, that I confess myself still undetermined. Y^r sou came to me teeming wth. all ye softer virtues: but then I thought, possess'd as He was of all ye Harmlessness of ye Dove, He still wanted some of ye wisdom of ye Serpent. And This, by y^e Œconomy of my Family, He will undoubtedly sooner acquire here than at Home. But, how will you forgive me sh^d. I suffer Him to lose in Gentleness, Simplicity, & Inoffensiveness, as much as He gains in Address, Prudence, & Resoluⁿ? And I must assure you f^m. Experience, that This is a Dilemma by no means so easily avoided in Practice, as it may seem to be in Theory. Upou the whole, however, I can honestly give it as my Opinion (aud, as it must give you & Mrs. Washington much Comfort & Pleasure to hear it, I hope you will not suspect y^t. I c'd be so mean as to say so, if I did not think so,) that I have not seen a Youth that I think promises Fairer to be a good & a useful man than John Custis. 'Tis true, He is far f^m. being a brilliant Genius; but This so far from being considered as a Reflexion upon Him, ought rather to give you Pleasure. Parents are generally partial to gr^t. Vivacity & Sprightliness of Genius in th^r. children; whereas, I think, that there cannot be a symptom less expressive of future Judgment & solidity; as it seems thoroughly to preclude not only Depth of Penetration, but y^t attenⁿ. & applicaⁿ. w^h are so essentially requisite in ye acquisiⁿ. of knowledge. It is, if I may use ye simile of a Poet, a busy Bee, whose whole Time passes away iu mere Flight f^m Flower to Flower, with^t rest^g upon auy a suff^t. Time to gather Honey.

He will himself inform you of ye accident He lately met with; and as He seems to be very apprehensive of y^r. Displeasure, c^d. I suppose it necessary, I w^d. urge you & his mamma to spare Rebukes, as much as he certainly deserves Them. Mrs. Washingtou may believe me that He is now perfectly well. He seem'd to xpect me to employ a Doct^r. but as He met wth. ye accident by his own Indiscreⁿ. & as I saw there was no Danger, I thought it not amiss not to indulge Him. The calling in a Physician upou any trifling Occasion, I think, is too likely to render Children needlessly timorous & cowardly.

I did not misunderstand ye meaning of y^r. Request, in ye matter wherein you suspect I possibly might; being persuaded that you know as well as I do, that such particular Attention is not only unnecessary, but impracticable. He will probably iuherit a much more cousiderable Fortune, than any other Boy here; and I thought it by no means an improper or unreasonable Request that a p'ticular atten^n. sh'l be bestow'd on a youth of his Expecta^{ns}. But as any Partiality to Him on ye trifling Circumstances of his Diet or other accommoda^{ns}. w'l. be rather disserviceable to Him than otherwise, I have taught Him not to expect it. The only p'ticular atten^n. you c'd. wish for. I also think Him entitled to; & that is, a more vigilant atten^n. to ye Propriety & Decorum of his Behav^r, & ye restrain^g Him f^m many Indulgences, w^h. I sh'd. willingly allow p'haps to ano^r. Boy, whose Prospects in Life do not require such exalted sentim^{ts}. Y^e allowing Him more frequently to sit in my Company, & being more careful out of ye Company of Those, who might probably debase or taint his morals. Had I my choice, believe me, it w'l. be more agreeable to me to superintend ye Educa^n. of two or three promis^g Lads, than to lead a Life of ye most voluptuous Indolence: but the Truth is, oblig'd as I was to engage in it by necessity & not by choice, I have often found myself so ill-requited, & ye office itself considered as so low, & so often taken up by ye very lowest Fellows one knows of, that, after hav^g laboured in it for upwards of seven years, with^t hav^g added much either to my Fortune or Reputa^n, I am almost resolv'd to drop it entirely. Yet whilst it continues to be agreeable to you to let Mast^r. Custis remain with me, it will be a Pleasure to me to have ye managem^t. of Him: nor can I indeed come to any decisive Resolu^n. as to ye other matter, till I know more certainly ye Fate of my Expecta^{ns}. in Maryland.

Be so obliging as to find some speedy & safe conveyance for a L^r. to Mr. Addison, w^h. I take ye Liberty of recommend^g. to y^r p'ticular Care, as it might be of much Detriment to me, sh'd. it fall into ill Hands, as has been ye case once before.

I beg Pardon for this very tedious Letter, w^h. I have tax'd you wth. ye Perusal of, and, wth mine & my sister's compt^s. to Mrs. Washington, I am &c.

Boucher to Washington.

Dear Sir,   CAROLINE, 5 September, 1768.

I was much concern'd for Mast^r Custis's Indisposition, w^h yet I foresaw, & sh^d have told you so, as I did Him, had I not been unwell at ye Time He left us. He is fond of Fruit, & w^t is worse for Him. He is fond of cucumbers; & to These, I doubt not, in a g^t measure, He owes his bilious complaints. A better air, & stricter attention, I trust, will soon restore Him to his former Health.

I did intend to have dismiss'd my Boys a week ago; but th^r Parents & Friends hav^g neglected to send for Them, many of Them have had, & still have this vile Disorder. And as both my Sister & Usher are also down in it, I see no chance I have of quitting ye Place during ye sickly season, w^h was my chief aim. Thank God, the Fevers are not very obstinate this year, & easily give way to Vomits and Bark.

Unless you hear from me again, I shall be glad to see Jack here ag^n ab^t ye latter End of this month, if his Health will then permit Him: & I hardly expect He will be in a Capacity to leave Home much sooner. Then, I hope, he may come without Danger. Mr. Addison is expected here every Day, who will probably either come or return your Way.

I beg my comp^{ts} to Mrs. Washington & her son, & am &c.*

---

* "December 16, 1768, Jacky Custis came home from Mr. Boucher's."—*Entry in Washington's Diary.*

Boucher to Washington.

FREDERICKSB^c, 11 January, 1769.

Dear Sir,

I have been much concern'd that it has not been in my Power to spend a few Days at Mount Vernon, as I hop'd I should. A very painful Disorder I labour'd under when Mast^r Custis left me, confin'd me to my Bed a Fortnight; and now it is too late to set out, when I expect all my little Flock to return immediately, as some of Them already are. You will please therefore to let Mast^r Custis know, that it will be to no Purpose for him now to wait for me, as we proposed when we parted; & that I shall expect to see Him at St. Mary's, as soon as ever a good Day or two may tempt Him to set out.

If Mr. Magowan be still with you, be so good as to enquire if He rec^d a L^r f^m me ab^t a month ago: The Parish In Louisa I mentioned to Him is still vacant, tho' warmly sollicited for by his Fellow-Candidate Mr. Contes & others. I am &c.

Washington to Boucher.

MOUNT VERNON, 24 April, 1769.

Your favor of the 17th came to my hands this day; the contents of which, or the Letter itself shall soon reach Mr. Addison's hands. In respect to the Dancing Gentry, I am glad to find you have such a choice of them, and that Newman has got the start of his rival Spooner, because I have heard him well spoken of as a teacher in that science. The other's misfortune might recommend him to the notice and charity of the well disposed, but if his accomplishments in that way are inferior to the other's, it ought by no means to entitle him to the preference. You will be so good, therefore, sir, to enter Master Custis with Mr. Newman for a year or otherwise as he may form his school. Mrs. Washington I can venture to assure you, will be very glad to see you at Mount Vernon in the recess of Whitsun Hollidays, but it is a pleasure I must be deprived of, as I expect to be in Williamsburg before, and long after that time.

Washington to Boucher.

MOUNT VERNON, July 13th, 1769.

Revd Sir

As we have fixed upon the 27th Inst^t for our departure to the Frederick Springs, & Mrs Washington is desirous of seeing her son before she leaves home, I am now to request the favour of you to permit him to come up for that purpose so soon as this letter gets to hand (by Mr Stedlar, which I am told will be eight days after date).

Nothing new in this part of the country worth a recital, and therefore I have only to add the comp^ts of Mrs Washington and my own to yourself & Miss Boucher, and our Loves to Jacky.

I am, Revd Sir, y^r most H^ble Servt.*

* A copy of this letter was courteously sent to me by Mr. R. F. Sketchley, in charge of the Forster Collection, South Kensington Museum.

CAROLINE, 20 July, 1769.

Sir,

In consequence of your L^r. Mast^r Custis now waits on you; & as this is a pretty busy Time with us in school, I shall be glad He may set off back again at ye same Time you do for the springs.

Enclosed you have his acc^t for ye last year, which as you were so obliging as to offer me when I was at Mount Vernon, I will beg ye Fav^r of you now to send by Jack.* I hope it will not appear too high to you; it being just what I charged ye only Boy (Mr Turner) I ever had living wth me in ye same manner he does. For my own Part, I must own to you, I charge his Horses merely by Guess, hav^g never very nearly attended to ye Expence of maintain^g a Horse: Those I have mentioned ye matter to here, think it too low: you, probably may have had occasion to consider ye matter, therefore I beg leave to refer it entirely to y^{r}self. I have yet to mention to you on this subj^t that, perswaded by my own Experience, I have lately come to a Resolu^n of tak^g no more Boys for less than £25 p^r ann: There are now four upon these Terms, & more expected soon. Unless therefore you object to it in Time, you must expect next year to find your son charged so too.

I have a Pleasure in informing you that I please myself wth think^g we now do much better than formerly: You will rem^r my hav^g complain'd of Jack's Laziness, which, however, I now hope is not incurable. For I find He will bear driving, which heretofore I us'd to fear He would not. He has met wth more Rig^r since I saw you, than in all ye Time before, & he is the better for it. This I mean only as to his Books; in other matters, He is faultless. His new Boy too is infinitely fitter for Him than Julius: & if He be not spoil'd here, which, in Truth, there is some Danger of, you & He & I too will all have cause to be pleas'd at his having made ye Exchange.

Miss Boucher was very intent on going to the springs, but being now convinced that she cannot, consistent with associa^n Principles, she is contented to drop it. She begs her respectful comp^{ts} to Mrs. Washington & Miss Custis may be join'd to mine, heartily wishing them as well an agreeable Jaunt, as that They may reap all the Benefit they xpect from the waters. I am &c.

I had forgot that the Dancing school is to be at this House next Friday. He has already miss'd two, & sh'd not therefore, I think, neglect attending this.†

Washington to Boucher.

4 December, 1769.

" Jacky will inform you of the Reasons why he brings not the Books you wrote to me for, and to him I refer. Perhaps all, or most of them, were included in the catalogue I sent to England for him, and if so, I expect they will be in, in less than three months.

" The Printer has promised to have a Musick Book rul'd for Miss Boucher if I come up, if so it shall be brought. Jack's stay has been longer here than we intended, but we hope he will endeavour to make atonement by extraordinary diligence."

* July 20, 1769. Paid Rev. Mr. Boucher, for schooling and Board of J. P. Custis, serv^t, horses &c.^{s}, £42, 1, 11.—*Ledger entry.*
† Washington went to the Springs July 31 and returned in September.

Doctor Cooper to Doctor Boucher.

KING'S COLLEGE, NEW YORK, 22 March, 1770.

My dear Sir,

I hold myself much obliged to you for good will, as well as good offices, towards this college, as instanced in your Conduct respecting Mr. Custis; and I am under still weightier obligation, when I consider your very friendly suspension of Belief, with Regard to some Reports, which you tell me have been circulated in your Parts to our prejudice. I am conscious that we have Enemies in abundance—that every Dissenter of high principles, upon the Continent, is our Enemy—that many of their missionaries, from the northern into the southern provinces, make it their Business, nay, have it in Charge from their masters, to decry this Institution by all *possible* means; *because* they are convinced, from its very Constitution—being in the Hands only of Churchmen;—which is very far indeed from being the Case of any other college to ye northward of Virginia,—and I know of none to the southward of it—they are convinced that it must eventually prove one of the finest supports to ye Church of England in America.

Hence there arose an opposition coeval with ye College itself—or rather, with the very first Mention of an Institution so circumstanced; which hath been continued, without Interruption, to this very Day, with much Resentment, Inveteracy, and Malice. The College of New Jersey—and those of New England—were already in their own sole Directions, and yet they could not be satisfied that ye poor Church should have any Influence in *one;* not that Dissenters of any Denomination are excluded from either Learning or Teaching; nay, we have educated *many*, and have several at this very Time, who do Honor both to us and to themselves.

However, oweing to the very Opposition, or to our own Care & Circumspection,—which may, perhaps, have arisen from the former,—our Numbers yearly increase, and our present apartments overflow. It would ill become any one, to boast of the advantages enjoy'd by a Seminary over which he himself presides: but I will venture to affirm, that, with Respect to *Discipline* (which, it seems, is one heavy accusation exhibited against us) we are far from being outdone by any College on the American Continent: and I *know* of none in Europe, to which, in this article, we are really inferior. Add to this, that the Expence—however such Things may be magnified by our adversaries, is not half so much as at any of the latter; and, I believe very little, if at all, more, than at *most* of the former. Our Tuition is only five pounds—one Dol^r passing for 8 shillings—New York currency: Room rent four; and Board, including Breakfast, Dinner and Supper, at ye Rate of eleven shillings a week, for ye Time each student is actually in College. These (saving Firewood, Candles & Washing, which must be had everywhere,) are the principle Expences, indeed almost the only ones, of the truly collegiate kind. *Others*, indeed, *may* run higher—as in Dress, and *sometimes* in Company, than they do at Colleges in the Country; tho' even these will not be materially different to a student of *real Gentility:* For such a one will chuse to appear handsomely-habited in all situations; and when he *does* go into Company, he will chuse the best for his associates.

With Regard to our plan of Education, it is copied, in the most material Parts, from Queen's College in Oxford; with the wh[ole] system of which, (having been for many years both Learner and Teacher in that seminary, with the character of which you are by no means unacquainted,) I looked upon myself as perfectly familiar.

The young Gentleman's Guardian may rely on everything in my Power for his Ward's Emolument: but as to my turning *Private Tutor* as it were —it seems to me so inconsistent with my office (whatever others in my situation may think of it) that I must beg to be excused. But I repeat—That I will shew Mr. Custis every mark of care & attention, and see that his other Teachers shall do the same.

I have only to add, that I *wish* he may be here in June,—as we do not admit pupils when absent.—that I beg my best Respects to Col". Washington, whom I shall be exceedingly happy to wait upon in New York (yourself, I hope, in Company)—and that I am, D' S' Y' Aff" Friend

and very obed' servant, &c.
M. COOPER.

I hope you will have patience with me—at present I suffer much by a severe fit of the gravel.

Boucher to Washington.

Dear Sir, CAROLINE, 2 April, 1770.

I felt so strongly the Truth of your Remarks, that I took shame to myself for having reduc'd you to so distressing a Dilemma. Believe it, however, sir, that it was Necessity, & not Inclination, that urged me to the step, which yet I sh'd hardly have taken, at last, cou'd I have supposed the circumstances of Mast' Custis's Est" to have been as you represent Them.

I have now the Pleasure to inform you, that I trust my present Difficulty will be surmounted, with' laying my Friends under a contribution. I am almost sure it will, if Mr. Claiborne will only be punctual in paying his £50, which I was Security for. A Debt, of long standing, & which I had almost despair'd of, fortunately for me, has just been paid: & This, with some collections I have made from the Est" of a deceased Friend, on w" I administered, have enabled me to make up my Sum of £200. this last, indeed, was an Expedient I very unwillingly had Recourse to; but I now learn by Experience, that real Distress is very effectual in teaching a man to get the Better of cert" delicate Qualms of conscience—& let This teach me to view, w'" candor, the Peccadillos of others in similar circumstances. I purpose replacing This with what I am to receive of you on Mast' Custis's acc', &, therefore, if not highly inconvenient to you, wou'd this year prefer a Bill to Cash, and shou'd I again be obliged to call on you before it is due, as I hope I shall not, I flatter myself with being again excused.

Might not your proposed Improvemen" of y" Naviga" of the Potomac to the W:ward be accomplished on some such Plan as This?—I mean by obtain" an Act of Assembly, empowering cert" Commissioners therein named, to borrow the Sum supposed to be wanted at a high Interest (suppose 10 p' cent) & this Interest to be rais'd f" a Tax proportioned thereto, on all y" vessels mak" Use of s" Naviga"? Or, if y" Naviga" w" bear it, w" tho' p'haps it might not at first, yet, undoubtedly it soon would, might not this Tax be rated so, as to produce a considerable Surplus, enough not only to sink the original Loan, but to raise a Fund for still farther Improvem". Are not some of the canals in Engl", & y" Turnpikes on this System? &, if I mistake not, the very grand canal now carrying on in Scotland is so too.— You doubtless have heard long ago w' was done on this matter by the Maryland Assembly; but, as I fear, f" y' acc' of Things, our Assembly w" not easily be persuaded to advance any cash towards the scheme, tho' I can have no immediate Interest in it, I s" be grieved so beneficial a Project shou'd be dropp'd.

I guess my Friend Mr Addison met with some Difficulties in y[e] Bargain he pro[mised] to make for me, as I have never heard from Him, nor about the Boy.

Custis who, as well as myself, is but just return'd from a Trip I took Him into Richmond County, is gone to write to his Mamma, to whom, & to Miss Custis, with many thanks for the[r] obliging Helps to my Garden, I beg my affectionate compliments. I am &c.

Boucher to Washington.

CAROLINE, 9 May, 1770.

Sir,

There are some particular Circumstances in my affairs, at this Juncture, which make me desirous to know your & Mrs. Washington's final Resolution respecting Mr. Custis's visit to Europe. Should you think it advisable for Him to go, & I be thought a proper person to accompany Him, I still am willing to do it, & on Terms which, I can hardly think, you will judge unreasonable.—I do not mean to take upon me to advise you in the matter; yet, I cannot help giving it you as my opinion, that, from what I know of Him. Travelling will be of peculiar Service to Him. And, as he is now advancing fast to that period of Life, much the most hazardous, this Expedient, if ever adopted at all, should be resolved on early, and put in Execution, at least, in two years from this Time. The Expecta[n] of it will engage his Attention, & divert Him from what I think a very wrong System, tho' a very common one, with the Youth of Virginia; it is to be hoped too, that it will stimulate Him to pursue his Studies with greater Earnestness, when he recollects how often He must be put to the Blush, if he appears illiterate amongst Men of Letters, into whose Company, in Travelling, He will often fall.

Surely, it will not be thought that I can possibly have any interested views in this matter. It is true, indeed, I wish to revisit my native Country; and I have too a strong inclina[n] to see the diff[t] parts of the world. In point of Prudence, however, I believe it were better for me to remain contented as I am; I consider it in this Light, that I am unconnected in the world, with no very violent Passion, but that of increasing my slender stock of knowledge, which I persuade myself I shall most effectually accomplish by a Tour thro' those Countries where Arts & Sciences have been most successfully cultivated. These, believe me, are all the interested motives I feel the Influence of; & if I have either heretofore or now, recommended it to Mr. Custis to travel, it was from a full conviction how necessary & how useful it w[d] be to Him. I have many Reasons for this opinion, some of which, I believe, are not unknown to you.

Happening, at present, to be a good deal hurried, I have only Time to add, that I wou'd by no means have mentioned this matter to you now, had not my own affairs required it; & that I can never consent to his leaving Virg[a], unless He is first innoculated, which therefore should be resolved on as soon as ever you can be advis'd of a good opportunity.

I beg my respectful Comp[ts] to Mrs. Washington & Miss Custis, & am, very truly &c.

P.S. I have shown Jack what I have wrote, and desir'd Him to think of the Project calmly & coolly, & then sit down, & write you fully his own sentiments on the Subject.*

---

* Washington's answer to this letter is printed in my *Writings of Washington*, II., 277. On May 20th Washington noted in his Diary, " Breakfasted at M[r] Boucher's."

Boucher to Washington.

St. Mary's, 21 May, 1770.

Sir,

So hurried as you know me to be at present. I flatter myself you will not even now expect more of me than the Outlines of a Plan of Travelling; the filling it up may be the work of further Leisure, & maturer Consideration. And, as I have nothing to lay before you, but mere conjecture & opinions, unsupported by any Experience of my own, let me again have Leave to remind you not to pay any greater Deference to These, or to any Opinions, than They are found fairly to deserve. It is a Project of suff^r Importance to warrant y^r collect^g ye Opinions of all who may be suppos'd to have ever attended to, or tho't of the matter.

Travelling. you are well aware, is still & long has been much in Vogue in our Mother Country; yet has it so frequently been attempted & executed in so absurd & preposterous a manner, that it is now become a Question whether it be really useful or not. And as warm an advocate as I profess myself for this method of complete^g an Educa^n, I yet readily own that it is only some Persons to whom Travelling can possibly be useful, & that there are perhaps equally many to whom it w^d certainly be pernicious. The light, giddy, fantastical, frothy & frivolous characters amongst us, w^d only be made worse, & rendered incurable; but let sedentary men talk as much as they please of ye Loss of Time, ye Expence, & ye unsettled & roving Habits acquired by Travel, to me it is beyond a Dispute, that an observant mind, & to a Person endowed wth Judgment to draw profitable knowledge f^m ye various objects w^h various Countries are perpetually present^g, there is not ano^r so eligible a System to be taken to form & polish ye manners of a liberal Youth, & to fit Him for ye Business & Conversa^n of ye world. And if you will be pleased to apply this Remark to some living Instances to be met with even here, I am mistaken if it will not account for that Objec^n so often started by the Opposers of this Plan,—that such, & such an one have travelled without being any better for it. Depend upon it, they were either originally unfit for the Experiment, or it has been conducted on wrong Principles. Let this be s^d with^t any suspicion of my aim^g to reflect on any Individuals; the Reflection is not confined to Virginia. But there is a cert^n captiousness in some of y^r Countrymen, w^h I cannot but lament, tho I very freely pardon as being but ye Ebullitions of Zeal for th^r Country, w^h will hardly allow a Foreigner (& such I must be called, in spite of my sincere attachm^t to Virg^a & Virginians) to find Fault with any Thing belonging either to Them or to their Country. But, as I am well convinced this is not ye Case wth you, I return to my subject.

It being then agreed, at least by you and me, that generally speaking, travelling is useful & necessary, to young Persons in all Countries, let us, as more immediately interesting us, now more particularly enquire, if it be not particularly so to a Virginian and to Mr. Custis. The peculiar advantages w^h result to youth from Travel, are s^d to be first, an easy address, ye wearing off of national Prejudices, & ye find^g noth^g ridiculous in national Peculiarities; &, above all, that supreme accomplishment w^h we call a *Knowledge of ye World*, a science so useful as to supersede or disgrace all ye Rest: for I understand not ye Phrase in ye Sense in w^b Fops or Rakes use it, but mean by it that easy, that elegant, that useful knowledge, w^h results f^m an enlarged observa^n of Men and Things, f^m an acquaintance wth ye customs & Usages of various & distant Countries, f^m some Insight into their Policies, Governm^t, Religion & Manners; in a word, f^m ye study & Contempla^n of men, as They present Themselves on ye gr^t stage of ye World, in various Forms, & under diff^t Appearances. This is that Master Science which every G—man sh^d know, & w^h yet no School nor College can teach Him. To apply this to ye Country we live in, where will you point out to me another so circumscrib'd in its Intercourse wth mankind at large, as Virg^a? Saving here and there a needy Emigrant from G^t Britain, an illiterate Captn of a ship, or a subaltern Merch^t, to whom can a Virg^a Youth apply for a specimen of y^r manners, &c., of any other People? Thus limited in ye Opp^{ly} for Observa^n must not his Ideas necessarily resemble those of a Caribbee Indian, mentioned by Lafitau, who, offended at being called a Savage, exclaimed, *I know no savages but the Europeans, who adopt none of our Customs;* or those of ye Inhabitants of the Marian Islands, who, being persuaded that theirs was ye only language in ye Universe, concluded from thence that all other men knew not how to speak? He finds his Lot cast in a Country amazingly fertile, & thence learns to conclude that even ye rich Plains watered by ye Nile, the Grecian Temple, the Roman Campania, the Spanish Andalusia, are all mean and contemptible w^n compared wth his *low Grounds;* &, pursuing this Train of Reasoning, soon supposes also like the Baron of Thonderton Tronck, that both his country and countrymen, are the finest of all possible Countries & People. Now, if it were only for ye sake of Truth & Decency, if it were but to avoid ye Ridicule to w^h these palpable Absurdities expose them, one cannot but wish our Youth c^d be taught to open th^r Eyes, & extend them beyond their own foggy air & dirty acres. But, This is not all: there is not a country in ye World, where a Man of capacity c^d be more eminently useful by promot^g & encouraging ye Arts, than in Virg^a. Till very lately you cou'd hardly anywhere see a piece of Land tolerably plough'd, or a person who c^d be persuaded that plowing made any difference; & even yet it is more than probable, even Those who have made the greatest Improvements in this most natural, most useful, & most amusing Art, fall infinitely short of some other countries. In a political View then, Travelling appears to be exceedingly necessary; since a Man may thus learn to double the Value of his Estate.

I mention'd too ye Improvem^t of Manners; by w^h I mean an Ability for ingenious, manly & useful Conversa^n. For a Traveller who makes a proper Use of his opportunites, will be all of a piece, & return as polished in mind & understanding, as in his Person. To this it is frequently objected y^t w^h is gained in Civility & Politeness, is lost in real Goodness & Virtue, by ye various tempt^g scenes of vice to w^h a youth must be exposed in ye Course of his Travels. In Aus^r to This, let me observe that there are some Tempers who c^d not possibly be preserved f^m ye Taint of Vice, even wth ye benefit of a private Educa^n. Or grant it were practicable to retain ye Purity of their Morals by such narrow Regula^{ns}; do not you think that if, by this Means, They sh^d chance to have fewer vices, They w^d also have fewer Excellencies? And it sh^d be remembered that solitary virtue, however pure and immaculate, is but imperfect virtue: We are formed for society, & ye Business of ye World is a Duty we owe to society: & it is therefore our Duty to qualify ourselves for ye performance of these Duties in ye best man^r, w^h is by prudent & well-conducted Travel.

Let us now, if you please, as a contrast to This, for a moment figure to ourselves future History of our pupil, sh^d this Expedient not be approved of. The chief failings of his character are that He is constitutionally somewhat too warm—indolent & voluptuous. As yet these Propensities are but in embrio : ere long, however, they will discover Themselves, & if not duly and carefully regulated, it is easy to see to what They will lead. At best, He will soon lose all Relish for mental Excellence. He will unwillingly apply to any Improvem^{ts} either in Arts or Sciences. Sunk in unmanly sloth, his Estate will [be] left to ye managem^t of some worthless Overseer; & himself soon be entangled in some matrimonial adventure, in w^h as Passion will have much to say, it is not very likely Reason will be much listened to. I appeal to you, sir, if this acc^t be exaggerated; & if it be not sadly verified by many living Instances y^t have fallen under y^r own Observaⁿ.

The Contrast is so striking to me, at least, it seems so, that I cannot think it possible for any one to hesitate a moment in determin^g. Let me then hasten just to repeat w^h. I yesterday mentioned to you of ye manner in w^h. I cou'd wish my scheme to be executed. In the first Place then, I wou'd have Him make the Tour of N. America, at least ye Northern Colonies, w^h. might very well be done in six months. And this chiefly to avoid ye absurdity of going so far to get acquainted wth other Countries, ere He knew any Thing of his own. After this, He sh^d go to Engl^d., & there immediately be enter'd in one of ye Universities, not so much f^m. any Prospect of advantages to be gain'd by study in ye little Time He c^d. stay there; as that it would be by much the safest Place for Him. After a winter or so spent there, He shou'd be conducted thro' ye principal counties & Towns of the three kingdoms, which wou'd possibly take up nearly a year. After this, He might conveniently spend six months in the metropolis, & from thence set out on his Tour thro' some of ye principal countries on ye continent. w^h. He sh^d. travel tho' not as a virtuoso to collect Rarities, or as a connoisseur, to gaze at excellent pictures or magnificent Buildings, but rather like a Really sensible & *sentimental* Traveller, such as Horace intimates Ulysses was, who travell'd thro' many cities to see ye manners of many men.—These are the Outlines of my Plan, which however I no otherwise recommend to you, than as my first thoughts, w^h. I shall be proud to see improv'd by y^rself or others. The Expence of the undertaking yet remains to be spoken of, in estimating of which, I am even more at a Loss than in what I have heretofore mentioned. However, as I had much rather have my Judgm^t. called in Questⁿ. than my Inclinaⁿ to comply with every Request of yours, I hesitate not to give you my Opinion such as it is. I cannot then believe that it can possibly be executed in any such manner as you w^d. wish, or as it ought, for less than £1000 sterl^g. p^r. ann: if so little; which I calculate in this manner. It cannot be tho't unreasonable that my appointm^t, if finally I sh^d. be pitch'd upon to accompany Him, sh^d at least be equal to w^t I relinquish here; as I take not into acc^t ye Injury I may thus eventually do to my future Prospects in Life, since This I think, ought to be charged to ye Pleasure I propose to myself f^m ye scheme. This then I set down at £250; my Expences & those of a serv^t & a p^r of Horses, at as much more: His own, & serv^t &c. at £250—the remaining £250 I allot to cloath^g Him, & sundry other unforeseen Expences, such as Purchasn^g Curiosities, visit^g public Places, &c., &c. For aught I know, this may be too much—tho' I hardly think it is: shou'd it be so, as I know his circumstances, it sh^d be my study to proporⁿ his Expenses, as far as they possibly could, to his Income. And whoever be his Precepter, sh^d have it strictly in Charge punctually to render you a faithful acc^t of every Disbursem^t, that so you might have it in y^r

Power to subject Him to whatever new Regula^{ns} you might judge expedient.

I am much ashamed to lay before you so confused & ill-digested a Letter, w^h I beg you to impute to my Hurry, & my being constantly interrupted by company: If, however, you can only collect from it ye substance of my Plan, & if that only appears tolerably plausible to you, I am not very anxious for ye rest, relying so entirely as I do, on y^r Candor to excuse any Inaccuracies you may meet with in w^h I have wrote. This only I have to request of you, that w^n you consult any of y^r Friends on this matter, you will be so good as not to produce this Letter, which tho' I am not afraid to trust you, I am yet unwilling sh^d be perused by strangers.

As to M^r. Custis's living wth me in Annapolis, shou'd I resolve to remove thither, as I suppose I shall, I have not anything to add to w^h I yesterday told you. I purpose calling on M^{rs}. Washington in my way to Maryland, & shall then request Her immediately to write to you her sentiments, so that I shall hope to be obliged wth your final Resolution before I leave Annap^s, which will hardly be before the middle of next month. I am &c.*

Boucher to Washington.

ANNAPOLIS, 18 August, 1770.

Sir,

Jack comes a Day or two sooner than I intended, in Consequence of an Invitation from M^r. Galloway, & M^r. Magowan to go to West River, which he does this day. He brings you some samples, which I hardly expect will please. M^r. Anth^o. Stewart has a Cargo just arriv'd, not yet opened, in which, He says, are Assortm^{ts} of Coating: shou'd you rather incline to wait for a choice out of These, if you will be so good as to give me y^r Directions, I will endeavour to attend to them.—Their common Rate of selling, for ready money, is at 100 p^r cent, which I think is cheaper than with you. A Vessel will clear out from hence for London, in ab^t a week or ten Days. I will be careful of any Letters you may want to put on Board.

They are still going on wth th^r subscript^n for clear^g ye Potomac, &, as I am told, wth spirit. Four hundred pounds are subscribed in this City; nor have They yet got all They expect. Messrs. Jacques & Johnson set off for Frederick tomorrow, & talk of fixing a Day for a general meeting, before they return. Will it be convenient and agreeable to you to attend about a month hence, if you have notice in Time—at the spot, i: e: at, or near Semple's?

Dr. Ross yesterday shew'd me a Letter He had just receiv'd from Croghan at Pittsburg, which informs Him that a new Government is certainly determin'd upon in that western world—& that either Coll : Mercer† or one Mr. Wharton are to be appointed Governor. He speaks of its Boundaries &c. wth Certainty, as a Matter of Fact. Have you heard of it—& the Particulars? It will be an immence acquisition, if not immediately to the Wealth, certainly to the Strength of these Governments—& a fine Field for a project^g spirit to adventure in.　　　　　I am &c.

* A letter from Washington to Boucher, dated 30 July, 1770, is printed in my *Writings of Washington*, II., 283.

† Col. George Mercer, connected with the Ohio company.

Boucher to Washington.

ANNAPOLIS, 1 October, 1770.

Dear Sir,

I much wish'd to have accompany'd Jack, but cannot: & what is worse, we part on an Uncertainty, which may be disagreeable. I have some Thoughts for setting off for St. Mary's this week; & if I do get away, I can hardly expect to return again till I remove finally, which cannot well be sooner than the latter end of next month, so that, if I do not come by Mount Vernon, Jack needs not come hither, till you or He hear from me again.—A quondam schoolfellow of Jack's wrote to me last week to apply to Dr. Stephenson of Baltimore, to take Him to be inoculated. I have done so; & at ye same Time mentioned Custis to Him. He seem'd particularly desirous of having an opportunity of testifying his Esteem for you by shewing civilities to any person connected with you. And, cou'd you by any means resolve on this measure, I cannot but think the present a favourable Time, as there are now, or soon will be, many of his acquaintances there on the same Errand.

Probably, ere long, you will find out that He has lost his watch; & He deserves to be severely reprimanded for his carelessness. I have the watch, but do not care soon to put him out of Pain.

I heartily wish you an agreeable Tour thro' yonder Tramountain Regions, & am, very truly &c.*

Boucher to Washington.

ANNAPOLIS, 18 December, 1770.

Sir,

I thank you much for your Intimations respecting Master Custis. Were all those who have the Care & Direction of children as attentive to their real Interests, we should not have so many Complaints of children spoil'd by parental Indulgence.

It is not without much Concern I own to you, that your sentimts of this young Gentleman have, for some Time, been my own. I have observ'd his growing Passions taking this unpleasing Cast, without the Power of preventing it. To a youth, brought up in the calm, easy, & rational manner that He has, the ordinary means of violent Restraint or Controll, wou'd, I believe, rather defeat, than promote a Reformation. The system we set out with, that of tender persuasion, must still be pursued; and tho' it may not, perhaps, work a speedy cure, it certainly will in the End. I consider his rising Passions as some little streamlet, swelling by successive Showers, into something like a Torrent: you will in vain oppose its Course by Dams, Banks, or mounds: & the only certain means to prevent its becoming mischievous, is to lead it quietly along by a variety of canals, lessening its Force, by dividing it. There are but two cases in which I can foresee much real Danger to this young gentleman; & if He can be preserved from These I shall not be greatly apprehensive as to others. I mean his Love of Ease, & Love of Pleasure. Pleasure of a kind exceedingly uncommon at his years. I must confess to you I never did in my Life know a Youth so exceedingly indolent, or so surprisingly voluptuous: one wd suppose nature had intended him for some Asiatic Prince. Against these two insinuating & most dangerous Foes to all that is truly valuable in a

---

* A letter from Washington to Boucher, dated 16 December, 1770, is printed in my *Writings of Washington*, II., 519.

character, I have exerted all my opposition: and I trust not altogether
without success. For, in a contest of this sort, not to suffer a total Defeat
is in some measure to gain a victory. There is a Period in Life when these
Passions will wage a war with Reason; and, if you can but keep them [at]
a stand, perhaps a reasonable man will be contented. It could not be, but
that at one Time or other M^r. Custis must have been introduc'd into Life,
as 'tis call'd: and is it not almost too much to expect from one brought up
in so very guarded a manner as He has, that He should pass the fiery Trial
unhurt? He knows even now extremely little of the various Enjoyments
of social Life; & yet he is peculiarly susceptible of them. Is it not better
then, think you, that He sh'd be suffer'd occasionally to mix in Company,
unreserved, while He can have the advantage of a monitor at Hand, even
tho' He shou'd, as indeed is too often the Case, go farther than one wou'd
wish? It is, possibly, a misfortune to Him, that everywhere much notice
is taken of Him. Whether this may be owing to his Family, his Fortune,
His Manners, or his connexions, or all together, I will not now enquire:
But this is certain, that tho' I am often pleas'd with it, yet is it the source
of infinite Disquietude to me. It is here, as with you: He has many invi-
tations to Visits, Balls. & other Scenes of Pleasure, to which neither you
nor I can refuse his going—more especially, if we go ourselves. Indeed, I
do not know that it would be right to refuse, even if good manners wou'd
allow it. Yet so it is, He seldom or never goes abroad without learning
something I could have wish'd Him not to have learn'd. There are not,
that I know of, more idle or pleasurable People in Annap*, than there are
in any other Town containing an equal number of Inhabitants: yet some how
or other He has contriv'd to learn a great Deal of Idleness & Dissipation
amongst them. One inspires Him with a Passion for Dress—Another for
Racing, Fox hunting &c.—even the grave Coll. Sharpe, you see, led him
to talk of Guns & Rifles, with much more satisfaction than I can persuade
Him to talk of Books, or literary subjects. In Truth, it is one of the worst
symptoms that I know of in Him, that He does not much like Books: &
yet I have been endeavouring to allure Him to it, by every artifice I could
think of. I hop'd that cargo of Books wou'd have done it. Let me, however, do Him the Justice to own, that He has labour'd under some Disadvantages in this Place: my late unsettled manner of Living has been unfavourable to Him. He dislik'd the House we lodg'd at. & wth some Reason.
I cou'd not always be with Him. nor He always at his Book; & at such
Times, there was nobody in the House. with whom he could spend a leisure
Hour but tolerably agreeably. Unluckily too there lodged a youth with us,
of a character exactly calculated to spoil such a Lad as Custis. He is sensible, wild. volatile, idle & good-natur'd. You will know that I allude to a
son of M^r. Sam: Galloway's.* I by no means aim to reproach the young
Gentleman, whom really I like exceedingly myself. yet can I not help giving it as my Opinion that He has done your Ward more Harm than He or
his Family can easily make amends for. You cannot conceive wth w^t De-
light Custis w^d listen to his droll Tales, & acc^{ts} of his Pranks at school in
England.—There is another Particular too which perhaps Discretion wou'd
bid me suppress, but which I think I cannot honestly conceal from you.
Sam. Galloway has also a Daughter, young & pretty. Out of Respect to

* "I congratulate you on your success on the Falmouth turf. Our old acquaintance
Saml. Galloway retired from the Alexandria races, and from the pomp and vanities of
this world almost in the same instant—having taken his departure for the impervious
shades of death as soon as he got home."—*Washington to William Fitzhugh*, 11 November, 1785.

you. as I suppos'd, He frequently invited Custis to his House: it was disagreeable to me to be oblig'd to refuse Him, because it gave offence; but I believe He never was with her but twice—once when I was, & once when I was not. It was about the Time of the Players being here. Miss Galloway came to Town. Jack has a Propensity to the sex, which I am at a Loss how to judge of, much more how to describe. I observ'd somewhat of a particular attention, exceeding bare civility to this young Lady. I took such steps as I judged most likely to wean Him in Time—and it was done, I believe, effectually. I am asham'd to add, because it is but a mere conjecture of my own, & imparted to you in great confidence, that I cou'd not help thinking this gave some Disgust to the Family. I wou'd not willingly suspect People without Cause: but, however absurd & foolish such a Project must have been, were I to give you a Detail of all my Reasons, I am inclined to believe you wou'd think as I do. I am mistaken, if you or Mʳˢ. Washington have not also had an opportunity given you of penetrating thro' such a Design. There are here, besides me, who think them capable of it; tho' I do not know that there are any, besides myself, who have suspected them in this Instance. But be my suspicions well or ill-founded, I have very peremptorily refused an importunate application, repeatedly made to me since my last Return, to admit this sᵈ son of His into my Family.—Let me have leave to request, that these surmises of mine, which perhaps I have view'd in too serious a Light, may never transpire. I can hardly need to say to you, that were it known, I shou'd have the whole Family on my Back.

This is no pleasing Picture of his Conduct here: nor will it I fear, make you much in Love with his situation. I have so often said how unwillingly I shou'd part with the Boy, that I am afraid of being suspected of selfishness, if after this, I still advise you to continue Him. Yet I do advise you, &, if I know my own Heart aright, with the most cordial & disinterested sincerity. As I have already observ'd, he is now arriving fast to that Time of Life, when he must mix with mankind: This He can nowhere do without Danger; & I think He will be in less here, than almost any where else, and for a Reason which, did I not well know your Candor, I wou'd hardly venture to assign. Because, I believe, there is not (nor is it likely that now there ever will be), another Person, who has such Influence over him as I have. I hope I am not deceiv'd in the persuasion, that he has a very affectionate Regard for me: & I am sure I can have no motives that shou'd lead me to wish to deceive you, in assuring you, that not the least of his actions escapes my notice. I watch his every motion, & tho' he is perpetually doing something or other displeasing to me, yet, upon the whole, I still hope & believe, he will turn out, if not a very clever, what is much better, a good man. That he may, I shall not cease to use my best Endeavours, as well as my fervent Prayers.

I am aware of the Expensiveness of his living here: to lessen it in some measure, I have resolved to return his Horses back to you. He agrees they shou'd not be sent to Him till Easter: nor then, indeed, unless you hear more from us. Let us try what this winter's close application will do: We are now well fitted for it, & I think have a prospect of spending it as we ought. Let Joe bring back all his vols. of Cicero, Livy, & as many others as his Portmanteau will hold: as well as a small Parcel of mine, which he brought up from Mʳ. Brook's, when we last came from St. Mary's. I am &c.*

* Some letters from Washington to Boucher, written in January and February, 1771, will be found in my *Writings of Washington*, II., 313-319.

Boucher to Washington.

ANNAPOLIS, 11 April, 1771.

Dear Sir,

I do very cordially sympathize with Mrs Washington in the uneasiness I can easily suppose she must necessarily be under during this State of suspence. Her son was, last Monday Ev'ning, innoculated in Baltimore: and tho' there really be in his Favour Every Thing that could be wish'd for, yet, I know she will be anxious & impatient till it be over. All I can do to ensure Success she may depend on: & I can with Truth declare, that, at present, there is but a bare Possibility of his having it unfavourable. In Truth, They make so very light of it in Baltimore, that one is almost asham'd even to mention a Suspicion of a Possibility of Failure.—We went up on the Monday; & for Fear of his possibly catching it in the natural way, I had Him innoculated immediately; more especially as He was very eager for it, & in high Spirits. The Pill He took that night, made him a little sick; & Joe complain'd that His [   ] him very unmercifully. I left Him yesterday at the Doctor's, where every Thing seem'd agreeable to Him; & purpose being with Him again on Monday, as his Fever will likely be a coming on, on the Tuesday or Wednesday, & Eruption on Thursday: all which Time I will be there. The Doctor promis'd to write to you as you requested. And should any Occasion arise, you may depend on hearing from me, ev'n by Express: So that, if you do not hear from me to the Contrary, Mrs. Washington may rest assur'd all is well—as I give you my Word and Honour, that, if there be ever so distant an appearance of any thing unfavorable, I will not fail to communicate it to you immediately. There is a young Gentleman there (and but one, tho' more are daily expected) from Northampton County, of the name of Savage; a modest, well-behav'd man, & I believe the Clerk of a County there. He promised to be a Companion to Jack, and I dare say will be an acceptable one.

If any Thing should be the matter with Him, They are to send Express to me; and if they do, I shall have an Opp^{ty} of letting you know of it by the Post—if I do not, conclude all is well.—Shou'd I not write next week from Baltimore, which yet I intend to do, be not uneasy.—This will be brought to you by Mr. Templeman, & being written in a Hurry in a crowded Store, must, I fear, be confused. All I aim & wish is to make you & Mrs. Washington easy; & I hope you will be so, in Confidence that if there really were any Appearance of Danger, I wou'd not, from a mistaken Tenderness, conceal it from you.

I beg my aff^t Comp^{ts} (as Jack also did) to his Mamma, Sister, y$^{rse lf}$ & Mr. Washington, & am &c.

NOTE.—Washington's reply is wrongly printed in our *Writings of Washington*, II., 276, as having been written 29 April, 1770, instead of on the same date 1771. The copy sent to me by the courtesy of Miss Gutch, Norton House, gave 1770 as the year.

Boucher to Washington.

ANNAPOLIS, 19 April, 1771.

Dear Sir,

I feel much Heartfelt Satisfaction in having it in my Power to inform you that Mr. Custis is now out of all Danger of the Small Pox, in Dr. Stephenson's own Phrase. He cannot die if He would. I have been with Him all this week, & shou'd not yet have left Him, but that I knew you wou'd wish & expect an acc^t,—& I cou'd only give one, by coming down hither, to catch the Post that sets out this Ev'ning. Yesterday when He left Baltimore, no Pocks had appeared; & I was unwilling to write till I could have something more certain to say. This morning, I found three; & about five Hours ago, when we parted, I could but count Eight, which I believe will be his whole Number. His Fevers began on Monday, & were sometimes pretty high; yet never so much so as to confine Him above now and then an Hour or so to his Bed. In short, I think I have now seen better Authority than ever to say, that the Small Pox, in this artificial manner, is really nothing: its virulence is so abated & subdued, that I now no longer wonder to find men think so little about it as they do in Baltimore. And to me, the whole secret seems to lie in keeping them cool; Custis, I believe, has not been within five yards of a Fire, since he went to Baltimore. I sh'd wrong him not to add, that he has been exceedingly manageable, & always in spirits; much more so than his Countryman, Savage. The Doctor bestows many encomiums on Him: I believe He wou'd hardly have had one Pustule, had not the Doctor, at my Request, (for I thought, tho' in Point of real Usefulness, it seems it was a Matter of no kind of Consequence, his Mamma wou'd chuse He shou'd have some) given Him something warm to provoke Them out. Joe, I fancy, will hardly have one; unless the same means try'd this morning may bring Them out: it is however, quite sufficient that the Arm is enflam'd, and that He has had the Fevers. Jack's, as I remember, are one on his neck, another by his Ear, one on his Breast, two on one Arm, and one on another, and two on one Leg; not one on his Face. Ere I left Him, his Fever was quite gone, and I never in my Life saw Him better; so that I cannot but congratulate you & Mrs. Washington on this dreaded affair's being so easily & happily over.

He is not to be down till the Monday Sennight, which, I guess, will be about the Time of your setting out on your Trip downwards.

Dr. Stephenson desir'd me to apologize for his not writing to you, as being very busy, and not having any Thing very particular to communicate. His general Price is two Pistoles, & 25/ a Week for Board. I shall have occasion, next Week, to write more fully on this & other matters: at present, being a good deal fatigued & a little unwell, I beg leave only to add that, I am &c.

P.S. Wheat, in yonder busy Town I have just left, I think is 6/. Some days ago 'twas 6/3; & Flour, 16/. You know they have 112 lbs. to the Cw^t.

Boucher to Washington.

ANNAPOLIS, 3 May, 1771.

Dear Sir,

I have seldom found myself worse disposed to write, than I now am; being exceedingly displeased with Mr Custis, that, according to my express Desire to Him, He is not here Himself, to write & put both yourself and his Mother out of all further Anxiety on his Account. On Saturday last, He sent me word, he would come down on the Monday; but the Doctor being of Opinion that possibly he might give some Alarm to the People here, advis'd me to let Him remain a few Days longer. I did so; & it having happened that a Mr Gough, a Gentleman of Rank & Fortune, of his Acquaintance in Baltimore, was to be married either Yesterday or to Day, I take it for granted He has been prevail'd upon to stay on that Account. For I have seen a Gentleman of Baltimore, who tells me He was quite well on Wednesday. So that there wants nothing but Himself to say so, to put every Thing out of Doubt. And This being the Case, I guess you will continue to think it right still to forbear mentioning it to Mrs. Washington, till the next Week, when (shou'd He not have wrote you from Baltimore, as I hardly dare to hope He has), we will assuredly both write. In the mean Time, I thought it wou'd be more acceptable to you to have ev'n this imperfect Acc¹, than none at all. I am &c.

Boucher to Washington.

ANNAPOLIS, 9 May, 1771.

Dear Sir,

The Season of Suspense, I thank God, is now over: Mrs. Washington, without the Fears that would have been unavoidable during a State of uncertainty, will have the Pleasure of learning from undoubted Authority, that her Son is happily & easily releas'd from a formidable Disorder, without hardly one Mark to tell that He ever had it. He is as well as ever He was in his Life: indeed has such strong Symptoms of Health, as we almost find it inconvenient at this scarce Season of the Year, & dear Markets.

A Mrs. Buckner of the Parish I left in Virginia gave me a Power of Attorney to settle a Law-Suit she had won. I have agreed to take 50£ this Currency for her Claim, which Money is to be paid to my Order this Week in Baltimore, and out of it, I have ordered my Friend there to pay Dr. Stephenson's Acc¹, as well as some other little Claims Mr. Custis has left there. His Acc¹, I fear, will run high, as I see They have charg'd him at the Rate of 10/ a Week for the Pasturage of his Horses, & this in the Country; which I have refus'd to pay. He has also, very idly I think, exchang'd his Gray Horse, for a large clumsy black one, and is to give £4 Boot.—Having receiv'd Nothing from my Parish here, nor indeed being likely soon to receive any Thing; & as You may easily conceive that I have been put to pretty much expence, I begin to find it difficult to find Cash to support my Family. I have therefore thought of desiring the favor of you to pay this £50 Mary⁰ Curr⁰, in your Way up from W⁰ᵐˢburg, on my account, either to Coll: Jⁿᵒ Thornton, or, if you shou'd not chance to see Him, to Mr. James Maury, a Merch¹ in Fredericksb⁰. I hope this will not be inconvenient to you; &, after paying off all Custis's Acc¹ˢ, there will not be very much left for me, which however I'll be careful to acc¹ for when we settle. Exchange here, I am told, is at 66⅔, which will regulate your Paym¹ of this Money.

Sundry Papers have been put into my Hands by a Mr. Harrison, from some Person in England, attempting, in Consequence of an Advertisem¹ of yours in the English Papers, to prove his being true and lineal Heir to ——— Colville, to whom I think you were left Executor. I have promis'd to speak with you on the Subject; but as the Papers are bulky, shall forbear to send them, till your Return to Mount Vernon. In the mean Time, I hope They will not be excluded from their Claim, for want of asserting it in due Time.*

* It was the estate of Thomas Colville. Dr. G. Alder Blumer, of Utica, N. Y., has reprinted from Archæologia Æliana some curious letters on Washington's connection with this Colville estate, and has also printed the Wills of the Colvilles in full.

Mr. Johnson has also left with me another large Cargo of Physic for Miss Custis; of the Efficacy of which in working a total Cure, He seems unusually confident. This too I shall not send till you return.

A Letter for you, brought by a vessel to this Place, I take the Liberty of directing to you in Williamsburg.

You will not wonder that I request to know, as soon as it may be in your Power, what your final Determination is with Respect to this young Gentleman's going Home. On his Account, it were better to have it certainly known: & on my own, it is highly necessary. However eager my Inclinations might be for the Scheme, should it still, after mature Deliberation, appear to yourself & your Friends, prudent to be at such an Expense, I am not now sure it would be in my Power to embrace the offer. I am not indeed sure that I could resist; tho' it wou'd certainly be highly indiscreet in me to turn myself once more adrift into the wide world, without first securing to myself a comfortable Retreat. And I have not, at present, such fair Prospects as I thought I had, but a Week ago. There is a Parish vacant, not twenty Miles from Mount Vernon, where I shall hardly need to say, I wou'd rather be than any where else in Maryland. And I thought I had been sure of it: indeed I hope I still am, tho' the Governor says He expects from England a Schoolfellow & a Relation of his own to fill it up. If this Gentleman does not come in, which I fear may not be known for some months to come, I think I shall be appointed to it. And if I am, I flatter myself I shall, without much Difficulty, be able so as to settle Matters as to put it in my Power to pursue this favourite Plan: of which, however, it is but Justice to myself to own that, with Respect to myself, I am not nearly so anxious as I have been. Life wastes apace, &, unmindful of ye silent Lapse of Time, I have already trifled away but too great a Part of it: it is not therefore to be wondered at if, in my cooler moments of Recollection, I wish for a Settlement.

I beg your Pardon for all this Egotism, uninteresting to you: this week or two I have not been very well; &, if in this, & my former letters, I have been disagreeably troublesome, I trust you will be so obliging as to impute it to that Cause.

If it be at all inconvenient to you to pay this Money, on your Way upwards; or, if you may probably stay longer than June, I beg you to inform me; as I can then fall upon some other Expedient. I will also put your English Letter into the Post Office here, & hope they will forward it from Alexandria, without any fresh Corn.

I beg my respectful Comp^{ts} to Mrs Washington & Miss Custis; & am, Dear Sir, &c.

Posey, I hear, is in prison bounds.*

* John Posey, who a few days later wrote to Washington: "I could have been able to satisfied all my old arrears, some months agoe, by marrying old widow woman in this County. She has large some cash by her, and Prittey good Est.— She is as thick, as she is high, and gits drunk at Least three or foure a weak—which is Disagreeable to me—has viliant Sperrit when Drunk—its been Great Dispute in my mind what to doe—I beleave I shu'd run all Resks—if my last Wife, had been even temper'd women, but her Sperrit has given me such Shock—that I am afraid to Run the Resk again, when I see the Object before my eys is Disagreeable."—Queenstown, 25 May, 1771.

A Letter from Washington to Boucher, dated New Kent, 19 May, 1771, is printed in my *Writings of Washington*, II, 319 n. Another of 5 June, 1771, is in the same volume, p. 320.

Boucher to Washington.

Dear Sir,

I am sorry to have thrown any additional Difficulties in your Way, respecting the affair of Mr Custis's Tour. At the Time I wrote, Difficulties seem'd to be starting up before me, which I fear'd could not otherwise be remov'd, than by dropping all Thoughts of leaving Maryland. I wish'd from many Motives, to accompany Mr. Custis: it was, however, as you will readily allow me to declare, but the second wish of my Heart,—my first was, that I might be independent. After what I had already experienced, it wou'd have been terrible to have again thrown myself into the wide world, without having first secur'd a comfortable Retreat to return to. And, I fear'd, it was too much to ask both a competent Living, & such extraordinary Leave of absence. I have now, however, the very high Pleasure to inform you, that, with respect to myself, Things are much altered; and, if you [will] make it suitable in other Respects, I am willing & ready to accompany Mr Custis, on the proposed Tour,—I am at Liberty to add, on this Condition only, that we set out some time in the next Year. Contrary to the sentim^{ts} of my friends, who thought it better that I should first get my Induction into the Living I mentioned to you in my Last, ere I promis'd to make this other Request to the Govr, I resolv'd openly & candidly to lay before Him my real Views; with which he was so well pleased, as to promise me the Parish so soon as ever it was in his Power, & also Leave of Absence,—for one Year only at a Time, but renewable: an Expedient He is obliged to use, thro' a ffear of giving Cause of offence to the People here so unreasonably jealous of any Extension of Prerogative.—I have had much Talk with Him on the subject. He had often taken a particular notice of Mr. Custis, & on this Occasion, professes a strong Desire to oblige Him, and you: and, it may be, that I owe, in some measure, the exceeding obligegnesse He shew'd to me in this matter, to his Desire of being instrumental to the promoting a scheme He so highly approves of. It will be in his Power to give Mr Custis Letters, which may be very useful to Him; & this He will do with much Pleasure. In short, both He, and Mr Dan Dulany, with whom also, at your Request, I have convers'd on the subject, highly approve of the Project—*in Case, Mr. Custis's Estate will afford it.* I said, I believ'd it might be now worth £1000 or 1200 sterl^g p^r ann:, which Mr Dulany, judging from his own Experience wth his own son, thinks abundantly sufficient. Yet, he says, Experiences in Travel are so exceedingly vague, uncertain, & variable, that there is no ascertaining, exactly, what may be the proper Allowance. His son has cost Him from £100 to £1000. In Paris, I think, He says, He spent £500 in three months, besides the salary to his Tutor. Upon the whole, however, He is of opinion, that one year with another, Mr. Custis can hardly need to exceed the Income of his Estate.

In debating this part of the argum^t, it deserves no little Attention to enquire, how much of his annual Income He would probably expend, if He should continue these three years in Virginia. Living with you, or under your immediate Influence, He probably wou'd be restrain'd within proper Bounds; especially as I do not think He naturally is of an expensive Turn. But, I am mistaken, if, with the most rigid Economy, adapted to his Circumstances, He fell much short of what it will cost Him at Home, exclusive, I mean, of the Expence of his Tutor. And shou'd he unluckily fall into the Habit of dealing in Horses, or, but in a very moderate Degree, sporting as it is called, neither of which He could well avoid, from the general Prevalence of Example. I need only direct your Eyes to many young Gentlemen, of fair Hopes, so circumstanced, to convince you, that it is not likely to be much more costly to Him to spend these three perilous years abroad, than at Home.—But, what a Difference, my dear sir, in the manner of spending them, & in the Consequences! To me, it is so very striking, that I own I shall sorely lament if, with your very proper & right sentiments on the matter, any untoward Circumstances should yet arise from any other Quarter to prevent it.

I have, in many of my former Letters, already said so much on the subj^t of Travelling, that I am fearful of falling into Repetitions. I will only add now, what I do not recollect ever before to have mentioned, that it is more peculiarly necessary to Him, than most Youths I have known. He has that Placid Indolence of nature, Flexibility of Temper, in his mind & manners, which require some better knowledge of ye world, than He is likely here to acquire, to guard him against ye Consequences of too much Compliance & Confidence in the Generality of mankind.

There is, to a delicate mind, much force in some specious objections which you suppose may be urged, from the Consideration of your being but his Guardian. But, they vanish at the approach of fair Reasoning, as it were at the Touch of Ithuriel's spear. You are in Duty bound to promote Mr. Custis's Interest by every means in your power, & I am sure it is not more your Duty, than it is your Inclination. If, therefore, both yourself, and every other cool, dispassionate, & well-informed Friend be fully persuaded that thus alone you will most effectually promote his true and lasting Interest, ought you to be deterr'd by the vain Fears & mistaken Apprehensions of others? At this Rate, nothing good or great must ever be done in Life, & you have already far exceeded your Commission, ev'n with Regard only to this young Gentleman. I reason upon this, as upon ye other Occurrences of Life. I wou'd gladly do what, upon mature Deliberation & fullest Enquiry, appear'd to be my Duty; and if, after this, malicious or ignorant People wou'd still put an ill-natured or unfair Construction on my well-meant aims, I must be contented to bear it, as I do the other Ills of Life, as something that might vex me, but shou'd not make me very uneasy, nor unhappy.

Upon the whole, I do very earnestly wish, and, if I might have Leave, I would request, that this matter may, as soon as possible, be determined either the one way or the other. The next spring, if I recollect aright, is the Æra I always fix'd on for setting out; and there are many Reasons why it should not, and not one that I can recollect why it should be postponed beyond that Period. And, to me, as you will easily believe, it must be desirable, as well ind--ed, as essentially necessary, to know what is resolv'd on, as soon as may be. My little affairs will require some Time to put them into such a Posture, as I shall wish to leave them in; and, I suppose, it might be convenient to you too, to know certainly, ere you sent home this year's Invoice. If Mrs. Washington, & yourself, & his nearest Friends approve of it, there is little Likelihood, that the General Court will disapprove: would it not be a strange Exertion of Power if they should? Yet, it is right, they should be consulted, & their Consent obtained. Gov^t Eden strongly urges the Expediency of a six months' Tour thro' America ere he cross'd the Atlantic: it is certainly right, if for no other Reason, only that a man might not seem totally unacquainted with his own Country. Is it quite romantic in me to expect. that. possibly. you might find Leisure to spend a few months in our Party? April or May wou'd be about the Time for setting out.

I am much concern'd at your apprehensions of Mr Custis's slender Improvements. And. to shew you how thankfully I receive such notices, I will not deny, that, possibly, there may be some Foundatio^n for y^r fears, & that, morever. some part of ye Blame, possibly, belongs to me. I will go farther, & say that both He & I, as the K. of Prussia said, hereafter will do better. [ ] this, let me now have Leave to add that his Improvemen^{ts}, tho' not equal to what they might have been, are, I believe, not inferior to those of any other young gentleman so circumstanced. Nay, I will venture to say, He is a better scholar than most of his years & standing. He is not, indeed, as you observe, much farther advanced. than under Mr Magowan. I cou'd here say a good deal: let this suffice, that I hope He now knows. by just principles, what heretofore. he had acquir'd by Rote only. He has apply'd more closely of late. & has begun Arithmetic over again; & on his Return, is to enter upon French. There is a Deal of Difference to be observed in ye Educat^g a Gentleman, & a mere scholar.

You will receive Physic from Mr Johnson, & enclos'd, his Directions, as well as Dr. Stevenson's rec^t & mine. And the papers. respect^g ye Claim to Colville's Est^a, of w^h I beg y^r Care, as well as that you will. when in y^r power, direct me what ans^r to return to ye man, who put them into my Hands for you. I am &c.

In the Hurry of writing. I had well nigh forgot a Commission a Friend gave me to you. Mr Lloyd Dulany of this city is going to the springs this season. He understands you have a House there—if unoccupy'd & unengag'd, He w^d be much oblig'd to you for Leave to make use of it.

I saw Coll. Cressap yesterday. He seems quite confident the new Grant will take Place, & is taking his Measures accordingly. Govr Eden hears, that many of y^r Regulators have pass'd thro' this Province, & is surpriz'd Govr Tryon has not sent Expresses to the sundry Gov^{rs}, on ye supposi^n that they would.[*]

John Parke Custis to Col. George Washington.

ANNAPOLIS, 18 August, 1771.

My dear Sir,

I am exceedingly thankful for your Remarks on my Letter, which I am sorry to say, are but too just. It is however really true, that I was in a hurry, when I wrote: and though undoubtedly I might have found more time. I am obliged to own, that I am one of those who put off every thing to the last. And how it should or does happen I know not, but so it is, that tho I certainly can write as good English, & spell, as well as most people yet when hurried I very seldom do either. I might perhaps account for it in a manner less reproachful to me, but, as you have attributed it to Carelessness. alone, & as Appearances are so much against me, I suppose it is so. All therefore that I can now do is to promise to be more attentive & watchful for the future; your gentle, yet very striking observations shall have their due weight with me: they shall by no means deter me from writing to you every opportunity, & I desire you would whenever you find a mistake, point it out to me to the end, that by discovering my errors, I may

* A letter from Washington to Boucher, dated 9 July, 1771, is printed in my *Writings of Washington*, II., 329.

endeavour with more success to amend, and at length be capable of holding a Correspondence with you, more agreeable than at present, on account of my incapability. I am glad that Wells dealt with you, which may perhaps be a means of introducing your stock to a better market, & I think I may venture to say, you might were you to come over, find persons, who would give you 20/. I am sure they may afford it, when they can sell it again at 6 d p^{er} pound. Mr Boucher presents his Compliments to you & Uncle Bassett & kindly offers to your acceptance a Room in his House, it being almost impossible to get a Room at any of the ordinaries, the Rooms being pre engaged to their customers, which puts strangers to a very great inconvenience in attending the Races. Mr Boucher begs you would let him know as soon as you are certain whether you are a coming, or not, as he expects many acquaintances here at the Races whom he would be glad to serve should you not come.

> I am dear Sir your most affectionate
> & dutiful Son
> JOHN PARKE CUSTIS.

The Annapolis Races of 1771.*

Sept. 21.   Set out with Mr. Wormeley for the Annapolis races. Dined at Mr. William Digges, and lodged at Mr. Ignatius Digges.

22.   Dined at Mr. Sam. Galloway's, and lodged with Mr. Boucher in Annapolis.

23.   Dined with Mr. Loyd Dulany, and spent the evening at the Coffee House.

24.   Dined with the Govr., and went to the play and ball afterwards.

25.   Dined at Doctor Stewards, and went to the play and ball afterwards.

26.   Dined with Mr. Ridouts, and went to the play after it.

27.   Dined at Mr. Carroll's, and went to the ball.

28.   Dined at Mr. Boucher's, and went from thence to the play, and afterwards to the Coffee House.

29.   Dined with Major Jenifer, and supped at Dan'l Dulany, Esq.

30.   Left Annapolis, and dined and supped with Mr. Sam'l Galloway.

October 1.   Dined at Upper Marlborough, and reached home in the afternoon.

Boucher to Washington.

> ANNAPOLIS, 19 November, 1771.

Sir,

I have seen your Letter to your Son, & I will own to you, it has given me a sensible concern. That my Attention to him has not hardly been so close or so rigid, as I wish'd, or, as it ought to have been, is a Truth I will not attempt to deny. The Peculiarity of my Circumstances & Situation, as well as of my Temper & Disposition, are all I have to offer in my Excuse: which, however, I do not myself think to be sufficient. I know I might have Taught him more than I have, &, sincerely as I wish his welfare I wish I had: but I know also, that there are not many Masters under

* From an interleaved *Almanac* containing Washington's journal.

whom He would have learn'd more, than He has even under me. This Business of Education is a complex & extensive Subject: & a man should be well acquainted with it, before He ventures to pronounce how far another has, or has not, done his Duty. Dr Witherspoon, it seems, said I *ought* to have put Him into Greek. Now, how much Deference soever I owe to his Authority, I will venture to say, that this Declaration, at least, must have been made much at Random. It was not possible He should know what I *ought* to have done, from the few, & the Kind of Questions He ask'd. To be acquainted with the Greek is thought to sound well; but, to determine upon a Youth's literary Attainments from that Circumstance alone, is not, in my Judgment, a much wiser method than the vulgar way of enquiring *how far* a Boy has got; and if He has run thro' a long Catalogue of Books, to conclude He must be a good Scholar. Had Dr. Witherspoon been pleased candidly & fully to have examined this young Gentleman, I shou'd have had nothing to fear. He would not, indeed, have found him possess'd of much of that dry, useless, & disgusting School-boy kind of Learning fit only for a Pedant; but, I trust, He would have found Him not illy accomplish'd, considering his manners, Temper, & Years, in that liberal, manly & necessary knowledge befitting a Gentleman. I ever did hold in Abhorrence that servile System of teaching Boys words rather than things; & of getting a parcel of Lumber by Rote, which may be useful & necessary to a School-master, but can never be so to a Man of the World. In these, chiefly, Sir, your Son is deficient: & but that these are thought necessary to make a Shew of, it were not, I think, much to be lamented, should he ever remain so. I neither have attended, nor dare I promise that I can attend, to Him, with the Regularity of a School-master. But, Sir, tho' the little, unessential Minutiæ of School-Learning may have sometimes been neglected, and thro' my Fault; I think I know you to be too observant & too candid a Man to believe that He has been wholly unattended to. His particular Genius & Complexion are not unknown to you; & that they are of a kind requiring not the least Judgment & Delicacy to manage properly. Pardon me, Sir, if I assume somewhat a higher Tone in claiming some Merit to myself, for having faithfully done my Duty in this the most arduous, &, doubtless, by far the most important Part of Education. I have hitherto, I thank God, conducted Him with tolerable safety, thro' some pretty trying & perilous Scenes: &, remiss as I am, or may seem to be, I doubt not, in due Time, to deliver Him up to you a *good* Man; if not a very *learned* one. It will not be thought necessary for me to enter into a fuller Detail of this Matter: what I should say, I persuade myself, will occur to you.

Annapolis was as unfit a Situation for me as Him, which I knew not, till Experience told me. I am now, however, at length, again to return to the Country with a Prospect of fewer Embarrassments on my Hands, than it had been my good Fortune to be with out for these five Years. I once was, I think, a good Preceptor; I have never been so, in my own Opinion, for the Period just mentioned. If, however, you think proper to try me a little longer, I think I can & will do better for Mr Custis, than any other Man: if you do not think proper, convinc'd that you will be influenced only by your Regard for him, most ardently wishing that you may most effectually consult his Interest, I shall never blame you for removing Him — if, indeed, my Blame or approbation needed to be of Consequence to you. You will do me the Justice to believe that I can have no other Motive for wishing his Continuance with me, besides a Kind of an affectionate Attachment to the Boy, & a piece of Pride, it may be, that another shou'd not reap the Merit, if there be any Merit in it, of touching what I have begun. I am now, I trust, happily set above the Necessity of teaching for a livelihood; nor will I, as far as I can now judge, ever take Charge of another Youth besides the Three now with me. For the last year, I have long ago mentioned it to my Friends, I never intended charging either Custis or the other Two, any thing for Education; & this only from what I thought a Consciousness that I had not deserved it. If He continues with me & I do my Duty as I now intend (& if I do n[ot I will] be the first to tell you of it,) I will charge Him, at the least, four or five Times as much as I have ever yet done.

If, after all, you resolve in removing Him, all I have to add is a Request that it may not be to Princeton. Pay me the Complim' of believing that I know some thing of these Matters; and there is not any thing I am more convinc'd of, than that your own College is a better one — better in every Respect. You live contiguous to it, & hear ev'ry Objec'' to it, often magnify'd beyond the Truth; & were this the Case with Respect to the Jerseys, I am mistaken, if you would hear less there. If, however, the Objections to Williamsburg be insuperable, I wou'd then recommend New York; it is but a step farther, & for obvious Reasons, infinitely deserves the Preference.

I am, Sir,

Boucher to Washington.

Dear Sir, PRINCE GEORGE'S, 15 January, 1772.

I now take the Liberty of enclosing to you, Mr. Custis's Account for the Year & half that He has spent in Maryland. Undoubtedly, it makes a formidable Appearance, and, at first view, may go nigh to scare you; I cannot, however, believe, that, when you come to descend to Particulars, you will think it very extravagant, unless it be in the Article of Clothes, which He got by your Permission. I should, indeed, except out of this Remark, the Charge of the Man, at whose House we boarded; the highest and most unreasonable I ever paid in my Life. I am firmly persuaded, I never eat as many Dinners with Him, as He has charged me pounds; and yet no Deduction could I obtain for two or three Months of the Time, that I was in Virginia, & nearly as much that Mr. Custis was. You will believe that I disputed it as long as I could, but Custom was against me, & so, what could I do? There are, perhaps, some other Articles, a little in the Annapolitan Stile of charging: All I can say is, that I have been as careful of his Interest, as my own; & if, after all, his Bill be very extravagant (for I have of late, been so used to such, that I have almost forgot what is a reasonable one) you will do me the Justice to own, it is not from any Profits that have accrued to me. As many of these Bills as are undischarged, & totally out of my Power to discharge, an Attention to his Credit, as well as my ower, obliges me to remind you that unless it should happen to be inconvenient to you, I shou'd be much pleas'd to have it in my Power immediately to pay Them off. For what is properly owing to myself, it will be particularly agreeable to me to receive a Bill of Exch' on London, as I just about ower as much Money there, as I believe This will amount to. The State of Exch' here seems not to be nearly so determinate & fix'd as it is in Virginia; I inquir'd in Annapolis, last week, solely for the purpose of directing you in this Business; & tho' I met with different Informations, the most general Account was, that they did Business there at 55, which you will observe, I endeavour'd to attend to in my Acc^d, in reduc^g Virg^a into Maryland Money, which, yet, after all, may not be right. The Money He yet owes, charged in my Acc^t, you will see, is about £76; the Rest I wish you to give me a Bill for, which I reckon will be somewhat more than £50 sterling. I fear, I am not a very exact Accountant, not having been much used to such Business; you will therefore do well not to rely altogether on my Calculations, without examining them: I trust, however, there are not very material Errors. — I must not forget to let you know, that He just now tells me He owes a Silversmith an Acct., which, the Man being out of the Way, I could not get in, which he supposes may be 4 or £5, and some other little scattering small Debts amounting, He fancies, to 30/ or 40/. — If not disagreeable to you, I shou'd be glad these Acc^{ts} c^d be return'd; as I also am interested in some of Them. I have some others, not sent, in which things that He had are charged to me, & which has cost me no little Trouble to separate, and perhaps, after all my Pains, they are not quite exact. If it be necessary, you shou'd have these also, I will send Them. Some I doubt, I have lost; amongst which are L' Argeau's & Dr Stevenson, if perchance I have not already transmitted them to you. No Charge is made for his Education; and this not only because I was uneasy to see his Bill already run so very high, but also, because, as I have before intimated to you, my Attention to Him has not been so regular & constant, as that I could conscientiously make a Charge of it. For the coming Year, however, I purpose to charge Him ten, if not twenty Guineas; which lest you should consider as a Finesse, to make meamends for my Loss of the last year, I mentioned to you, that I might at the same Time inform you, Mr Calvert had agreed to give me that sum for his Son, but which, for the same Reason, I have not yet charged Him.—I know full well your Sentiments of my Conduct last year, & I honour you for them. It is a Subject I love not to think on, still less to speak or write about. Could I have foreseen how I shou'd live in Annap^o. He never shou'd have gone there with me: nor shou'd he have continued, but that I thought every Day, I shou'd certainly alter things, and live to myself. The Truth is, with many Demerits & Imperfections, I still love the lad, & as I cou'd not find in my Heart to part with Him, without an absolute Necessity. Thank God, it is now over; & tho', with my Acquaintances & Connexions, I never can be a very diligent Preceptor, yet I doubt not soon to make amends for all that is past. I have much Pleasure in informing you, that we all of us seem perfectly happy in our new Situation: it is quiet & comfortable, & I fondly hope, healthy. A *cruel something*, as Prior says, is, however, still wanting—this House is none of mine: but as I am now resolving in good Earnest to become frugal, I must comfort myself with the Hope, that I soon shall be in a Capacity to get one of my own.

Lord Baltimore is certainly dead. All that has hitherto been talked about his Will, is mere, random Guess-work. There are, however, some pretty good Reasons to believe, that the Proprietaryship of this Province, & the most considerable Part of his immense Property in the Funds, are left to the Family of our Friend, Govr Eden. The will, suppos'd to be his last, was in Naples, where he dy'd, Septr 4th., after a Fever of three Days, & not transmitted to England, when the only Let^r the Govr has yet rec'd from his L^{d}ship's Agent on this Subject, came away. Doubtless, this

Event will give Birth to many little Revolutions, of Consequence to us here. Most People I converse with seem anxious to have it confirm'd, that Mr Eden is Proprietor: Beyond all Question, it is the happiest Thing that can possibly befall the Province.

I enclose you some Proposals for a new Map of the Back parts of America. It was put into my Hands by a Friend from Philad. with a Request that I wou'd transmit it to you. Possibly, you know this L[ieut?] Hutchins, and can guess whether He is likely to play *Henry* with you. If I thought there was any Chance of its being well executed, I should like to subscribe. Shou'd it fall in your way to procure Him any Encouragement, you will hand his Paper about; & if you return it to me, I will take care to have it properly transmitted to the Author.

I beg my most respectful Compts to Mrs Washing. & Miss Custis, & am &c.

J. B.

Boucher to Washington.

21 February, 1772.

Dear Sir,

I congratulate you, & the world with us, on our Restoration to a temperate Zone: for, in Truth, we have had a kind of Greenland winter. And, for my own Part, I own to you, I now have a much stronger Idea, of the Nature of a Winter pass'd in a Cave, than I could ever have learn'd from Books alone. I sometimes almost regretted, we could not become quite torpid, & sleep out the whole dreary Season, as Snakes and some other Animals are said to do: or that, as, like Bears, we were shut up in our Dens, we could not, like Them also, live with out Fire, & by sucking our Paws: for I had some Cause to imagine, if the Weather had held much longer, we should have had some Temptation to try.

To what I have heretofore said on the subject of these Accounts, I have little now to add; unless, I should beg leave to suggest to you, by way of diminishing in some sort their enormous amount, that they take in a Period of eighteen months, at the least — & that they are in a Currency so much worse than yours. Comparing Him with the youths around Him, He really seem'd frugal; & as far as I know, never indulged in any expence that I could have suppos'd you would have had him restrained in. I knew you expected him to make such an Appearance as He did, & keep such Company as He did: I knew not of the twenty pounds, & am indeed somewhat surpriz'd at it: how it has been spent I know not. I have just enquir'd of Him, & can only hear that he bought Oranges & Pine apples, &c., and gave away a Ticket or two. But, as this is by no means a satisfactory Acct, I have ordered Him to write to you about it; & if he cannot account for it, at least to Apologize to you for his Remissness. I hope it was rather trifled & fooled away, than spent in a more blameable manner; which I think could hardly have been without my knowledge. And, a very few Venial Peccadillos excepted, I have little of this Sort to Charge Him with. The boarding a Person is not, I should imagine, to be considered as finding Him just such a Quantity of Provisions, &c. In Frazier's Case, it was his Livelihood, & a handsome one it is to him. He considers his House-Rent, & all his own Attendance, Servants, & a long et cetera. My Charge was governed by his, which, knowing my Board to be so much better, I thought a sufficient Warrant for me. I never aim'd to make a Living by taking Boarders: in Virginia, I am persuaded, I lost by it. You will, however, be so good as consider, that no Man can, even with the most easy & manageable Boarder, be quite so easy in his Family, as without Them — & something shou'd be allow'd for the Inconvenience He puts himself to. I do not, however, agree with you that £25 a year for a Boy in a kitchen, is an extravagant Charge: but, I suppose, it is considered as making some amends for other Disadvantages — at least, this was the Apology Frazier made to me.

I observe the Errors you have pointed out: in answer to which, all I can say is, that I well know I paid the Money to the Man, at the Time I have charged it: & This I am the surer of, as Mr. Custis also remembers it. Gassoway was represented to me as a Man who had once seen better days, & deserving of Compassion: He was exceedingly needy, & constantly sending to me for Money. How it has happened that He charged these Sums over again, & that I overlook'd them, I cannot account for, till I see Mr Jacques, who was so obliging as to take the trouble of settling with Him for Me. I will, however, have it rectify'd, & accordingly, I have already given you Credit for it in my Book.

I had much Trouble and Vexation in this said Country about this Article of Exchange: &, hitherto, have generally lost by it. They seem to have no standard, nor fix'd Regulation, as with you. I enquired of some of the Principal Annap[s] & Baltimore Merchants before I wrote to you: but, I will enquire again: & if Bills either have been, or shall be, either in this or the next Month, sold at 50 p[r] c[t], I will allow it. Some allowance you [think] is to be made for the medium thro' which one generally receives [   ]gence of this sort there are always a few degrees difference between a buyer and a seller.

I fear it will be impracticable to lay in Provender &c. for [   ] Horses in this neighbourhood: as I can hire but one Stable, & that a most wretched one. This Article, however, cannot possibly hereafter be so heavy a one as it has been — nor, indeed, I hope, any other.

L[d] B[altimore] is certainly dead: but, I believe it is still unknown [what his] Will is. It had not been sent to Engl[d] from Naples where He dy'd [when] the last Letters I saw or heard of came away. Every thing, however, known, is in favour of Gov[r] Eden. At all events, I guess, He [will not] have a fight for it: & I join with you in wishing that every [thing] may be as much to his Advantage as I shou'd fancy it is, that He [   ] possession. The chief Difficulty seems to be, whether the Proprietary [was] or was not entail'd, & so, whether willable or not. If this Doubt [can certainly] be answer'd in the Affirmative, I believe Mr Eden has little [chance] of being Proprietor. I have not seen him this Month, or upwards [   ] of trying to get thither next week, when I shall not fail to re[member you] to Him. Our Assembly, I hear, on Acc[t] of this desperate [   ] is prorogued till late in March. Shou'd I hear any thing that I can [   ] it wou'd be agreeable to you to hear of, I will write to you in W[ms]burg. I wish you a pleasant and agreeable Sojournment. I am &c.

I send back the Acc[ts], as I can do without them — & tho' I wish'd to have had Rec[ts] under them, yet, I fancy, my general Rec[t] may do.

Be so good as to take the trouble of two or three L[rs] to drop in your way down.

Boucher to Washington.

PRINCE GEORGE'S COUNTY, 5 March, 1772.

D' Sir,

At length I have seen an abstract of the will of the Lord Baltimore; more absurd & more vexing than you will easily believe. It appears to have been made fifteen months before his Death, in Venice, & is as follows:

To Mrs. Browning (sister of Mrs. Eden*) & Mrs. Eden,† each £10,000, on condition that they sign a Release to all Claim on the Province.

To Rob' Eden, Rob' Morris & busy Lawyer, & lately Secretary to the Society of the Bill of Rights), Hugh Hammersley (lately L' B———'s Steward or agent in England), Rich' Prevost‡ (his attorney, & of a good Character) Esq'', his Ex'', on condition that they prove the will within twelve months, each, £1500.

To Rob' Eden, one hundred pounds per annum.

To Henry Harford (a nat' son, ab' 15 years of age), the Province; Remainder to Frances Harford—§ Rem' to M'' Eden.

To Henry Harford, £30,000. Rem' to Frances Harford. Rem' to M'' Eden.

To Frances Harford, £30,000. Rem' to Henry Harford. Rem' to M'' Eden.

To M'' Hales (a woman whom he has been dragging round Europe, &, for a Lady of easy virtue, of good character), £1000.¶

To Two Miss Hales's (his Daughters by the above M'' Hales) each £2000.

Hen: & Frances Harford residuary Legatees.

I think I remember nothing more, & if I mistake not, you will think this quite enough. Two wills that he had left in England, in both of which, I believe, he had left* the Province, & the Bulk of his Fortune, amounting, it is said, to more than £100,000, were cancelled & destroy'd tho' there has not been known any Coolness between them, but on the contrary, an increasing affection, at least, in Professions. I am but little able to inform you what steps the Governor intends to take, tho' I happen'd to be with Him, when he received the will, only that He is resolved to try to overset it, & with good Hopes of success. They suppose the Province to be of that kind of Property which is not deviseable, contrary to the Opinion expressed some time ago, when there was no doubt but the will was in favor of M'' Eden, or her Family; & find Precedents in the case of the Duke of Athol with respect to the Isle of Man. In case of success, then, you see, the two sisters will be coheiresses, &, of consequence, M''. Eden comes in for but half, which, however, will be no contemptible Acquisition. You will readily believe how heartily I join with you in wishing success to this only Reputable Branch of a Family once so respect-

---

* Louisa Browning, Baltimore's eldest sister.
† Carolina Eden, wife of Robert Eden.
‡ Peter Prevost.
§ Henry and Frances Mary Harford were children of Baltimore by Hester Phelan, an Irishwoman. To Hester he left an annuity of £200.
¶ In the will, Mrs. Hales is described as "Elizabeth Dawson, of the county of Lincoln, spinster." The daughters were named "Sophia and Elizabeth." Boucher omits a member of a third denomination, "Charlotte Hope, daughter of a certain German woman called Elizabeth Hope of the county of Munster in Germany, an infant at the age of two months, more or less, and born at Hamburgh, the sum of £2000."

* To Governor or Mrs. Eden should be inserted here; though not in MS.

able: but, in Truth, their prospects seem sadly overcast; &, at least, they have a World of Difficulties to encounter.

If any thing that a wicked & a foolish Man does, cou'd justly be matter of wonder, this will wou'd really be unaccountable. Till now, this Boy was scandalously neglected: his Mother long ago displac'd on a very scanty Pension. Whilst Mrs Hales was thought to possess a plenary influence over him, was constantly with him, as well as her children.

I shall hardly need to say what Confusion this Event is likely to produce amongst us. The general Opinion seems to be, that the Crown, if not urged by an attention to the safety of the subject, yet as constitutional Guardian to the illegitimate Boy, will immediately appoint to the Government. The northern Papers, I hear, have already mention'd Mr Zachary Hood, the Man that came in here as Stamp Master, for the Gov^t. I think it far more probable that your Friend Coll. Mercer will be the man: unless Governor Eden & his Friends shou'd apply, which hitherto he seems by no means determined upon. It certainly is, by no means, a very romantic Conjecture, to imagine that we shall now ere long become a royal Government: a Revolution, but little wish'd for by the people here.

I hardly ever have seen a Man bear the shock of ill news with such composure as the Governor; undoubtedly, nothing was remoter from his Expectations, than so absurd & reproachful a Distribution of so immense an Estate, which he had been repeatedly assur'd wou'd belong to his Family. Mrs Eden indeed is more affected. She may well, having been tormented by him thro' the whole Course of her Life, &, at last most villainously dup'd & cheated. Cajoled by his specious Assurances, the Govr was tempted to give up his Prospects in the Army, which were flattering; & Mrs Eden, decoy'd hither, greatly against her Inclination. It is happy for them, that they have [   ] & comfortable Competence to retire to, fortunately out of his Re[nts.]

The Govr begg'd me most cordially to thank you for your friend [   ] & to assure you of his great esteem & Regard for you. I expect [   ] next week, & had you been at Home, we shou'd certainly have [   ] other tempted you to join us. He has got you a very handsome & [   ] whale Boat, for £20, which, I fancy is by this Time at Mount [Vernon].

I beg the Favour of you to speak to your two Printers, & [   ] my Newspapers, if by this Time, I owe them for a year. I shall [   ] also, you will be so good as remind them to direct for me to the care of [Mr. Lowndes] Merch^t in Bladensburg, as I have hardly seen one Virginia Paper since Xmas. Purdie & Dixon will oblige me by sending me the address of the Clergy [   ] ward, & Dr. Chandler's appeal, & G Watkin's Ans^r, &c., which I have seen advertis'd by Him.

I hope to see you in Maryland soon after your Return, & in the meantime am &c.*

Boucher to Washington.

22 May, 1772.

Dear Sir,

I send Joe over on purpose to let you know that the Govr & Mrs Eden will not wait on you this Trip: some unforeseen occasions call them again to Annap^s sooner than they expected: they therefore desir'd me to beg your excusing them at this Time. They still talk, if it be practicable,

---

* Letters from Washington to Boucher, dated 4 and 21 May, 1772, is in my *Writings of Washington*, ii. 347, 349.

that they will visit you before M[rs] Eden leaves the Country; but, of this shou'd I chance to get notice, as I probably shall, I shall find occasion hereafter to inform you. The Gov[r] dines with y[r] Neighb[r] M[r] Digges tomorrow, & sleeps at Mr. Roger's, where I am again to meet Him. Shou'd you be quite at Leisure, & your whole Boat be arriv'd, perhaps you may be tempted to try her. 'Squire Calvert alone accompanies Him. Mentioning this Gentleman's Name, reminds me of a Request he made to me, that I wou'd engage of you for Him & myself, thirty or forty Weathers, for Muttons, in the next Fall, if you shou'd then have so many to spare. I beg you to attend to this, & to give us the Preference to any other chap: we will hereafter contrive about getting them over, if we can but have them.—I forgot too, in my L[r] by Peale,* to tell you from Mr. S. Galloway, that he had sent you two Cases of excellent claret (I have tasted it, & it really is good) to Mr. Ignatius Digges's. I think each case contains 6 Doz:, & I believe at 45/ p[r] doz: I guess you will have it carted down to Piscat[y], & fetch it thence by water; & if I can be made assisting to you, surely you will not hesitate ab[t] command[s] me.

With this vile Pen & ink, even were I not exceedingly hurried I have some doubts whether you will be able to read what I attempt to scrawl. I will not therefore add a word more but that I am &c.

Boucher to Washington.

CASTLE MAGRUDER, 19 January, 1773.

Dear Sir,

It is certainly expedient to remove M[r] Custis to some Place of publick Education, and speedily. And where there is so noble, so princely an Institution of this sort, in his own Country, it is lamentable to find there still should be a Necessity for sending Him to another. I had, as you know, been endeavouring to believe the many Stories we are perpetually hearing of the Mismanagement of W[m] & Mary as partial & exaggerated: but, the Carefulness of your Enquiries on the Spot excludes all further Doubt about the matter.

I can truly say, I do not differ from you in Opinion, but with diffidence of the Rectitude of my own; nor wou'd I venture to mention my differing with you at all, had I not long ago experienced your Candor in allowing for the prepossessions or Prejudices of your Friends. I will therefore yet again take the Liberty of declaring my Opinion in favour of N. York, rather than Philad[a]. It is but justice to premise, that I am not personally acquainted either with the one Place or the other. You, I believe, are; & can therefore better judge, whether what I say on the Report of others be well or ill-founded.

Philad[a] is a large, populous, thriving, commercial City: & so is N. York. The Former, is this only; the latter is more. It is inhabited by [   ] People of the most considerable Rank & Fortune; it is a Place of the greatest Resort for Strangers of Distinction; it is the Head Quarters of the military; &, on all these accounts, is, I am told, generally reckon'd the most fashionable & polite Place on the Continent. As a Situation, therefore, for a young Gentleman, who is to be educated a little in the World, as well as in Books, it wou'd seem, that it deserves the Preference. In fact a little Residence in such a City is the best substitute I know of for the Tour that was once projected; as He stands a better Chance for acquir

* Charles Willson Peale, at this time painting a portrait of Washington.

ing that Liberality of Manners, which is one of the best Uses of Travel, by mixing occasionally with truly well-bred People. This, tho' I have not Leisure to pursue it farther, is of some Importance in the Determination of this matter.

Confident that my Letter is for, & will be kept to, yourself alone, I will not be afraid to speak out, tho' perhaps I may be mistaken, persuaded that I shall be pardoned, if wrong. I wou'd not rashly reflect either on any Bodies of Men, or Individuals; what, therefore, I am about to say, must be read with great Candor, and larger Allowances. From the best Observations I have been able to make on young Gentlemen educated in America, one general Fault is, that they come out into the World, furnish'd with a kind of smattering of every Thing, &, with very few Exceptions, arrant Coxcombs. Were it not too invidious, I cou'd name to you Individuals, who are really clever, but hurt one by this silly humour. And, I think, as many have brought away this sort of spirit from the Coll: of Philad⁴, as any other I have taken notice of. I know not a Fault one wou'd more earnestly wish to avoid; nor one, considering yᵉ Character & Manners of your Ward, that you shou'd more guard against. How far this may be owing to any peculiar Discipline, or Mode of Instruction in these Colleges, I presume not to say; certainly, however, the Fact is, as I have hinted, & I have heard the observation made by others as well as myself. That this is not also the Case with Respect to King's College in New York, is more than I have any authority positively to assert; I have, however, some Reason to believe, that it is not, at least not in so great a degree. Most other Colleges are formed on the Plans of those in Scotl¹, Leyden, Gottingen, Geneva; Wᵐ & Mary, & King's College, resemble more those of Oxford & Cambridge. In the former, Men often may become Scholars, if they will; in the latter, they must often be made so, whether they will or no. The Presid⁴ of the Coll: of Philad⁴, whose Abilities are unquestionable, was himself brought up in Scotland, in a less regular manner, than is the Fortune of Scholars in general; &, in spite of his great merit, this must be some disadvantage to Him in the office He holds. By dint of superior Genius, He has himself arriv'd at Eminence in Literature, by a nearer Cut, as it were; but, the Bulk of Men, must be enforced to travel thither, along the beaten Track. It is therefore, in some sort, necessary that He who undertakes to guide us, shou'd himself have travelled the Road He is to shew us. The President* of King's College is allow'd to be as sound & sensible a Scholar as any in America. He was first train'd up regularly in a large School in England, & afterwards completed his Education by a ten or twelve years Residence in Oxford. I do not, however, lay much stress on the comparative Merits of the Professors; both of those I have named possess extraordinary Merit. But, were the matter to be so determined, no Reason cou'd be given for his leaving his own Country, as I know very few better scholar's than either Mʳ [John] Camm or Mʳ Johnson.

It is but fair in me to advertise you, that I have, & long have had, a very warm & close Friendship with Dr. Cooper, Presid⁴ of the N. York College, that He is my Countryman, & constant Correspondent, & that, moreover, I am under some Obligations to the Trustees of his College for an honorary Degree, they were pleased to confer on me some time ago. How far, these Things may have biass'd my Judgment, you will judge better than I can. I profess, however, that I have not willingly suffered

* Dr. Myles Cooper.

private Friendship or Attachments to warp my
... suspect no ... inasmuch as I know, that the
Address, by far the best educated Man, & best his
Province, agree in this Matter, in Opinion with
Gentlemen proposes to give this ... young ... I
the Matter, the sending his own Son rather, ...
ever the ill-Health of Mr Addison shall permit
her. And I think I have heard Mr Walter ...
his youngest Son, that Mr Dunny is, I believe, a
... Relations there.

The Difference in point of Distance, I should ...
to deserve much Attention, even from a ... Fort-
Week, from the one Place as well as the other; &
... ought to be very frequent. a Day or two I
can make but little odd.

And now, my dear sir, relying on your ... ...
have been delivered with the best Intention, I
Determination of the matter, where doubtless it ...
with yourself. I have not now to inform you, ...
his Welfare, believe me, is the only motive that
Judgment; & were I not persuaded, that ... ...
promoted by sending him to York rather than Ph
the Liberty of troubling you with this long Letter

Whenever you have finally determined the mat
you to let me know; and, if it be for Philade
personal Acquaintance with Dr Smith, for whos
profess the highest Respect, I will give you the L

I have a Wish indeed, a strong ... to accompany
the Indisposition of my Eyes makes it almost ...
to seek assistance somewhere, & which, they tell
the Northward. But, whether I shall be able
order, as that my Absence so long may be leste
can now judge. This only I know, that it I ...

A very disagreeable Controversy, with two ...
which I was too easily persuaded to enter into, a
a good deal of Work. This, however, if other M
certainly not of moment enought **to** detain us.

Mr Boucher begs her aff Comp to Mrs Wash
which I request mine may be joined. I am &c.

    Boucher to Washington.
     Prince George's C

Dear Sir,

I hardly remember ever to have been more ...
days ago, on being informed by the Governor of
taken Place between Mr Custis & Miss Nelly Cal
to assure you, on my Word & Honour, that ...
the most distant suspicion of any such Thing; ...
me great uneasiness to learn, from the same ... to
in some measure to blame. To **this,** I can only r
the Error **was** of the Head, & **not** of the Hear

 * A letter from Washington to the Author, Boucher Curate
of Washington is 275.

the Justice to own. that I have repeatedly warn'd Him of the Hazard every man must necessarily run. who precipitates Himself into so important an attachment. ere the Judgment be fully matured. He has Reason to be thankful that He runs as little as any one can. The peculiar & extraordinary merits of the Lady He, fortunately, has singled out to place his affections on. assure me. he never will have cause to repent it, from Her: I wish, I cou'd be half so sure, that his own future Conduct & altered opinions, may never tempt him to wish. that He had let it alone, a little longer.

You will remember I always thought that he was enamoured of Miss Betsey; tho' even in that, I suspected not. that there was any Likelihood of its becoming so serious, without my first knowing more of it. Why, He has carried it so far, without ever deigning to pay me that common Compliment, which, I think, my Friendship for him well entitled me to, He best can tell. I will not. however. impute it to a worse Cause, than a false Shame. If he had consulted me, He would have found me in that, as I hope. He has, in other Things, candid and indulgent. But, when I recollect, that he neglected also to inform you, I forbear my murmurings, ashamed to insist too much on a Breach of Friendship, with your Example before me. who have forgiven a Breach of Duty.

I beg you to recall to your mind, what my Conduct has been in other Instances respecting this young Gentleman; and I am sure you will do me the Justice to own. that my not having advertis'd you of this also, has been owing solely to my not knowing it, myself. However infatuated I may have been in my political Pursuits, I would not have been wanting in so essential an Instance of Duty. I therefore. will hope. that you will not continue to judge harshly of my negligence. inasmuch as I again assure you, that. if I have been to blame. I have been so unintentionally.

I should belie my real opinion, were I not to say that. I think, it had been better for Mr. Custis not to have engag'd Himself; but, since This could not be. I should hardly belie it less, not to own, that I think he cou'd nowhere have enter'd into a more prudent Engagement. Miss Nelly Calvert has Merit enough to fix Him. if any Woman can; and I do, from the fullness of a warm Heart. most cordially congratulate his mother & yourself. as well as Him, on the Happiness of his having made this most pleasing of all connexions. with this the most amiable young woman I have almost ever known. I know her well. and can truly say, she is all that the fondest Parent can wish for a darling child. Warmed with the Ideas of her merit. I can almost persuade myself to believe, that the advantages which may be deriv'd to his Morals from this Engagement, rash as it has been, are enough to compensate for all the ill Influence it may be supposed to have on his intellectual Pursuits. There is a Generosity, a Fortitude. a manliness & Elevation of mind which such true Gallantry inspires. that is not so Easily otherwise taught. As I will not suffer myself to think. but for a moment. that He will ever be wanting in Honour or Integrity, so as to tempt Him to shrink from an honourable Engagement. I trust. He will also consider Himself as not less bound in Honour. to avoid all those sordid & less noble Pursuits, which wou'd debase. & render Him unworthy of Her. Nay, I trust that He will find himself enabled to collect the dissipated Powers of his mind, & apply with Earnestness to his Studies, which, it seems. He now confesses. He has not been able to do these twelve months. owing to the impression of this Passion. Upon the whole, it appears to me, considering his Temper &

MYLES COOPER DD. L.L.D.

Second President of Columbia College

Situation, his Friends have rather Reason to rejoice, than be uneasy at this Engagement.

I enclose you a Letter from Dr Cooper, which, I assure myself, will not be displeasing to you. He is a man of true merit, in every sense of the word; and you may safely depend on his Doing every Thing becoming such a man. You see, you have all this & the next month, before you; He should be there before their Commencement in June, that He may not lose a Term and, as his Friend & old Companion Carr, has some thoughts of accompanying Him thither, on the same Errand. I will be obliged to you, if, without Inconvenience to yourself, you can give Him three weeks or a month, to consult his Friends, & get ready.

I am told, you have Business to our Provincial Court, the next week; I hope to see you either agoing, or returning. The Govr. Mr Calvert, the Chief Justice, & Mr Dulany dine here on Monday. Should you set out on that Day, you know you can be here in Time to Dinner. I am, &c.*

Dr. Cooper to Washington.
KING'S COLLEGE, NEW YORK, 2 July, 1773.

DEAR SIR,

I rec'd your's the Day before Yesterday. Unfortunately, Mr Custis himself, having taken it from ye man employed by ye Post Master to carry Letters about, brought it to me; so that I gave the inclosed to him immediately, little suspecting the mournful Contents. The Shock, you may suppose, was severe; however, he is grown much more composed; & I hope his good Sense and Christian Fortitude, in a reasonable Time will perfect ye cure.†

He lives now altogether in the College, and dines with the Professors and myself in the College-hall. He has fitted up a Room in a neat, plain Taste, attends his Instructors punctually, and, I doubt not will make a Proficiency equal to ye warmest Wishes and Expectations of his best Friends. At present, indeed, as must be expected, his mind is not in a state to admit of any Intenseness of application; but I am persuaded, as his Grief wears off he will do every Thing that is reasonably to be expected from a young Gentleman in his situation. He has already gained much upon ye affections of his Instructors; which is a Circumstance that cannot fail of producing very beneficial effects, with Regard both to his Learning and Happiness, during his Residence in this Place.

I fancy he will not chuse to write to you himself for a few Days; but he has desired me to inform you that his situation among us is perfectly agreeable.

I have the Honour to be, good Sir,
Yr most obed' and obliged Serv' &c.,
M. COOPER.

John Parke Custis to Washington.
KING'S COLLEGE, 5 July, 1773.

Hon' Sir,

Pardon me for having thus impos'd upon your good nature by not writing to you sooner. I neither could nor had it in my power to say any

* Washington set out for New York on May 10th to place Custis under the care of Dr. Cooper. He reached that city on the evening of the 26th, and on the following evening was present at an entertainment given by the citizens to General Gage.
† "Patsy" Custis died on the 19th of June. A letter of Washington's to Burwell Bassett is in my *Writings of Washington*, ii. 384.

thing with certainty concerning my establishment here till now. It gives me Pleasure that I now have it in my Power to inform you how agreeably every thing is settled. There has nothing been omitted by my good Friend Doctor Cooper which was necessary to my contentment in this Place. And Gratitude as well as Truth obliidges me to say, that the other Professors are not the least remiss in their Duty but give all the assistance they can consistant with the Duty they owe to the other Students. I attend at stated Hours, the Professors, in mathematicks, Languages, moral and experimental Philosophy, & I hope the Progress I make in these useful branches of knowledge will redown not only to my own Credit, but to the Credit of those who have been instrumental in placing me here, & in particular render you some Compensation & Satisfaction for the parental Care and attention you have always & upon all occasions manifested towards me, & which demand my most grateful thanks & returns, to make which shall be the constant care of J. P. Custis.

I found great difficulty in disposing of my grey horse. His Colour made so much against him that I was obliidged (to avoid expence) to sell him at public Vendue for only 34 pounds this currency, a price tho below his value I was obliidged to take. The Bay I have kept & shall keep unless I hear from you to the contrary. He is a Horse I know to be good, & one I have a vast effection for, & except riding, there is no other exercise to be us'd here, which makes it necessary either for me to keep a Horse or hire a poor miserable hack to take an airing twice or thrice a week, the distance of 4 or 5 miles into yr Country for the Benefit of my Health.

There is nothing now, which interrupts my tranquillity, but the melancholy subject of your last Letter, & the uneasiness I fear my poor mother suffers on that account. I myself could not withstand the shock, but like a Woman gave myself up entirely to melancholy for several Days. I should most gladly have answered your favor when Doctor Cooper did, & have endeavoured to administer some comfort to my distrest Parent. But my Mind was too much agitated to admit a thought, & was illy capable to give others what it stood so much in need of it-self. But I am persuaded your Goodness left no stone unturn'd to render this shock as easy as possible, and I think the only & most effectual means to remove from her mind the Impressions of my Poor Sister, is to carry her from home for some considerable Time, for every thing at Mount Vernon must put her in mind of her late Loss. Should this thought of mine be approv'd of, the seeing of you at this Place would render me extremely happy, and answer fully the end of her Comeing. Doctor Cooper was speaking to me on this Head the other Day, & said then, that he would write to you to that effect, and recommend it as strongly as he could. If you should approve of this Scheme, & will let me know beforehand, I will exert myself in getting you Lodgings, & every thing else convenient. Dr Cooper has some thoughts of takeing a tour to the southward & of making you a visit this Fall, which if he does, I shall accompany him, as there is a Vacation then of four or five weeks.

Before I conclude I must beg you to write me immediately on the receipt of this Letter, as I am extremely anxious to hear how my mother bears this misfortune, & of your own Health, & be certain that I shall do every thing in my Power; to prevent your good advice being thrown away upon me.

I am with sincere regard & effection
Yours
JOHN PARKE CUSTIS.

Dr. Cooper to Washington.

Dr Cooper presents his most respectful Comp^s to Col. Washington; & returns him his Son-in-Law, without any Vices that he knows of, and with many Virtues, wherewith he is perfectly acquainted.

His assiduity hath been equal to his Rectitude of Principle; and it is hoped his Improvements in Learning have not been inferior to either.

KING'S COLL: NEW YORK
20 September, 1773.

Vardill to Washington.

KING'S COLLEGE, 20 September, 1773.

S^r.

I have taken the Liberty of addressing a Letter to you, on a Subject extremely agreeable to me, & which, I am sensible, must be particularly so to you. The Conduct of your Son, during his Residence at this Seminary, has been such, as that it would be injustice to deny *him* the tribute of approbation he deserves, & *you* S^r the satisfaction which a generous Parent must receive from the Reputation of one he loves. At a Period of Life in which the Passions are most violent he has discover'd a remarkable purity of morals, &, when Gaiety invited him to pleasure, has with such constancy devoted himself to his studies, as to give us the surest ground to expect that he will hereafter attain to that excellence, which his natural powers render him capable of. When I inform you, that his affability & Courtesy have endear'd him to mine, as well as to the affection of all who are concern'd in his Education, you may suspect me of partiality. But this Friendship itself would prompt me to the strictest sincerity in this Description, least I might injure one whom I esteem, by imprudently lulling Parental caution into a dangerous Security. If the Intrusion of this Letter wants an apology, I can only confess, that I could not deny myself the satisfaction of giving this testimony to merit, of presenting my humble respects to you, S^r, & your amiable *Lady*, of congratulating Her on the hopes that her Precepts & Examples of Piety will be practis'd & imitated by her son, & of professing myself, with all sincerity, S^r.

Your friend & humb^l serv^t

JOHN VARDILL.

Dr. Cooper to Washington.

KING'S COLLEGE, NEW YORK, 10 January, 1774.

Good Sir,

I have received yours and Mr Custis's Letters of the 19th of December. For the many polite Expressions of Regard, in Both, I beg Leave to return my just acknowledgments. I hope, and earnestly wish, the young *adventurer* may enjoy every Pleasure, in his new state, which his Imagination hath already formed; and, from every account of the young Lady's Disposition and Qualifications, and from my own knowledge of His, I cannot but think, that they bid very fair for Happiness: I pray Heaven they may obtain it.

The monies you left in my hands were nearly expended when Mr Custis went to Virginia: what remained not being sufficient to pay the Tutors the stipulated quarterly salary. Since the Rec^t of yours, I have called in all the Bills that I could think of; amongst which are *two* of considerable sums : viz. Rivington's of 19, 2, 3£ and Graham, a Taylor's, of £58 3 10½. Besides these there are several small ones; of all which, together with an exact account of my own Payments, you shall receive the sums, by the next Post; I say the *sums*, on account of the *postage*; the Bills themselves, as well as those already paid, with Rect⁵ to them, as those not yet discharged, being equally at your Service, if you think proper to have them.

The amount, taken collectively, seems large, but you will find, on Consideration, that yᵉ really collegiate Expenses are no ways high. The death of Miss Custis brought on a considerable charge; but then the articles are in Being. The Chair, the Horse, the Money given to Mʳ Custis for travelling Expences swell the Bill exceedingly; but then the two former articles are nearly worth as much, I presume, at this Time, as they were then. The money laid out in papering the Room &c., *may* be sunk of course: the furniture has been sold at auction, under the care of Mʳ Harpur, into whose Hands Mʳ Vardill committed the Business, upon his sailing for England. The same person has packed up Mʳ C's Clothes, &c., & sent them as directed. You will find that yᵉ professors have just been paid their constant Wages; with which they have no Reason to be dissatisfied; though they much lament Mʳ Custis's unexpected Departure. For my own Part, it is impossible to make any charge at all; I have no Idea of it.

I should have been happy in waiting upon you at Mount Vernon; but circumstances, not to be foreseen, utterly put it out of my power to begin my Journey, till such Time as I was convinced you must have set off for Williamsburgh: so that I was not *disappointed*. Perhaps upon some future occasion, I may be more fortunate. It would afford me much pleasure to spend a few Days with you and Mʳ Custis *any* where: and, I hope it is not unsupposeable that you and He (after he has been some time a Husband) may take another Journey to the Northward.

I will write to Mʳ C. when I send the accounts. In the mean Time I beg my best Regards to Him, & am &c.

M. COOPER.

You must excuse the *scrawl*; for the Ink, every second, freezes in my Pen.

Dr. Cooper to Custis.

KING'S COLLEGE, NEW YORK, 5 February, 1774.

Dear Sir,

I did myself the Pleasure of writing to Colo. Washington yᵉ 10ᵗʰ of last month, and promised, in that letter, to write to you, & send the state of your accounts, by the next week's post.

My Intention was good—but I *could* not act up to it, as the accounts could not so soon be collected. I have, now, I hope, got them all. I do not send them inclosed, on account of yᵉ postage: but Mʳ Harpur, who knows much more of Figures than myself, has taken the Trouble to digest them; and in such a manner as, I hope, will make them intelligible enough, to a person skilled in Business at least, however they might perplex one unused to such like Transactions.

I am apprehensive the sum of them rises higher than your expectation: I own it is higher, by much, than *I* supposed it *would* have been. *Graham's* Bill is an *heavy* one, but *you* best know what articles you had of him. I always heard him reckon'd a *dear* Fellow—as I once told you;—whether he is honest or not, is another Question : But it is certain he is a violent presbyterian.

You will, I hope, not take it merely as a compliment—to which kind of Business you know I am not much addicted—when I assure you of my being very sensibly affected upon your leaving this College. The Regard I had conceived for you, from the Regularity of your Conduct, and the Goodness of your Disposition, could not possibly produce any other effect upon me. However, I doubt not, from ye amiableness of your *Lady—that is—or Lady-that-is-to-be's Deportment,* Character, and Accomplishments, that she will make you happy *at home,* which is more than most people, I fear, find themselves to be *abroad.*

Our good Governor is very much indisposed ; &, I presume, will hasten away to England with all possible expedition. Miss Bell Auchmuty, I hear, is on ye point of marriage, to a Mr Burton, an English Gentleman of considerable Fortune, settled at Brunswick. This is all the news I *recollect.* Indeed, my Hands are so full of Business since Mr Vardill's Departure, that I cannot often stir abroad, add to which, that, for upwards of a week past, I have been much indisposed with a most violent cold, as not to be able to leave even my Room.

What is become of Mr Boucher? I wrote to him, presently after my Return from Maryland ; but not one word have I heard of him since. I hope you will not be so totally engaged, after marriage, as our Friend seems to have been.

With my best wishes for your Happiness, and my best Respects to Col^o Washington, whom, you know, I highly esteem, I am, dear Sir, &c

MYLES COOPER.

Boucher to Washington.

THE LODGE, 6 August, 1775.

Dear Sir,

I thought it far from the least pleasing circumstance attending my removal hither that it placed me in your immediate neighbourhood. For having now been happy in your acquaintance several years, I could not help considering myself, nor indeed help hoping that I was considered by you, as an old friend ; and of course I counted on our living together in the pleasing intercourse of giving and receiving the mutual good offices of neighbourhood and friendship.

That things have turned out much otherwise I need not inform you. Mortified and grieved as I confess myself to be at this disappointment, I am by no means prepared to say that you are wholly to be blamed for it ; nor, as I would fain hope you in your turn will own, is it entirely owing to any fault of mine. I can easily suppose at least that we neither of us think ourselves to blame ; and yet I cannot help thinking that had I been in your place I should, in this as well as in other things, have taken a different part from that which you have chosen. Permit me, sir, as one who was once your friend, and at any rate as one not likely to be soon troublesome to you again in the same way, once more as a friend freely to expostulate with you. If I am still in the wrong, I am about to suffer such punishment as might satisfy the malice of even the most vindictive enemy ; and if you are wrong, as in some degree, I think you are, it is my duty frankly to tell you so, and yours to listen to me with patience.

On the great points so long and so fruitlessly debated between us it is not my design now again to solicit your attention. We have now each of us taken and avowed our side, and with such ardour as becomes men who feel themselves to be in earnest in their convictions. That we should both be in the right is impossible, but that we both think we are we must in common candour allow. And this extreme difference of opinion between ourselves, when we have no grounds for charging each other with being influenced by any sinister or unworthy motives, should teach us no less candour in judging of and dealing by others in a similar predicament. There cannot be anything named of which I am more strongly convinced than I am that all those who with you are promoting the present apparently popular measures are the true enemies of their country. This persuasion, however, will by no means justify me, should I be so weak and wicked as to molest them while they do not molest me. I do not say this because I happen to be in what is called the minority, and therefore without any power of acting otherwise: it is the decision of truth and justice, and cannot be violated without doing violence to every system of ethics yet received in any civilized country. The true plan in such cases is for each party to defend his own side as well as he can by fair argument, and also, if possible, to convince his adversary: but everything that savours of, or but approaches to, coercion or compulsion is persecution and tyranny.

It is on this ground that I complain of you and those with whom you side. How large a proportion of the people in general think with you or think with me it is in none of our powers to ascertain. I believe, because I think I can prove it, that your party, to serve an obvious party purpose, exceedingly magnify the numbers of those whom they suppose to take part with you, and you tax us with doing the same. But there is this great, manifest, and undisputed difference between us. No Tory has yet in a single instance misused or injured a Whig merely for being a Whig. And whatever may be the boasted superiority of your party, it will not be denied that in some instances at least this has been in our power. With respect to Whigs, however, the case has been directly the reverse: a Tory at all in the power of a Whig never escapes ill treatment merely because of his being a Tory. How contrary all this is to all that liberty which Whigs are for ever so forward to profess need not be insisted on; it is so contrary to all justice and honour, that were there no other reasons to determine me against it, as there are thousands, I would not be a Whig, because their principles, at least as I see them exemplified in practice, lead so directly to all that is mean and unmanly.

It is a general fault in controversial writers to charge all the errors of a party on every individual of that party. I wish to avoid the disgrace of so indiscriminate a judgment; and therefore have a pleasure in acknowledging that I know many Whigs who are not tyrants. In this number it is but doing you common justice to place you. I wish I could go on, and with equal truth declare that, whilst you forbear yourself to persecute your fellow subjects on the score of their political creeds, you had been as careful to discourage such persecution in others. Scorning to flatter, as much as I scorn to tax you wrongfully, I am bold thus openly to tell you I think you have much to answer for in this way. It is not a little that you have to answer for with respect to myself.

You know, and have acknowledged, the sincerity and the purity of my principles; and have been so candid as to lament that you could not think on the great points that now agitate our common country as I do. Now, sir, it is impossible I should sometimes avow one kind of principles and sometimes another. I have at least the merit of **consistency**; and neither in any private or public conversation, in **anything I have** written, nor in anything I have delivered from the pulpit, have I ever asserted any other opinions **or doctrines than** you have repeatedly heard me assert both in my own house **and in** yours. You cannot say that I deserved to be run down, vilified, **and injured in the** manner which you know has fallen to my lot, merely because I cannot bring myself to think on some political points just as you and your party would have **me think.** And yet you **have borne to** look **on,** at least as an **unconcerned spectator,** if not an abettor, whilst, **like the poor frogs** in the **fable, I have in a manner been** pelted **to** death. **I do not ask** if such conduct **in you was friendly; was it** either **just, manly, or** generous? **It was not; no, it was acting with all the** base **malignity of a virulent** Whig. **As such, sir, I resent it; and** oppressed and overborne as **I** may seem **to be by popular obloquy,** I will **not** be **so wanting in** justice to myself as not **to tell you, as I now do** with **honest boldness, that** I despise the man who, **for** any motives, could be **induced** to act **so mean a part. You are no** longer worthy of **my friendship; a** man of **honour can** no longer without dishonour be **connected with you.** With **your cause I renounce you; and** now for the last **time subscribe myself,** sir,

Your humble servant

JONATHAN BOUCHER.*

Boucher to Washington.

PADDINGTON, NEAR LONDON, 25 May, 1784.

Sir,

I will not affront you **with any apologies for this intrusion; for, greatly** altered **as I am to suppose you are, since I had the Honour of living in** Habits **of Intimacy with you, it is not possible, you can** be **so changed as that you would not feel** yourself **hurt, & with Reason, were any man, who had** ever **known you, to** think it necessary **to apologize** to you for doing which he is prompted to do, only, by a sense **of Duty; &** what, moreover, He believes it to be **no less** your Duty **to attend** to, than it is his to suggest.

It is no Part of my present Purpose to trouble **you with** any Reflections **of mine on the many great events that have taken Place within** the last

<hr>

* This letter was furnished, with other material, to the *Notes and Queries*, 5th series, vi, August 26, 1876, by the grandson of the writer, Rev. Jonathan Bourchier. In the same periodical (5th series, ix, 19 January, 1878) Col. Joseph Lemuel Chester, by no means an unimportant authority on questions relating to Washington, raised the question whether the letter had ever been received by Washington, and believed that the dedication of the "View of the Causes and Consequences of the American Revolution" was a complete withdrawal of the "unfounded charges" made in 1775. There is certainly no record of its reception by Washington, but it does not follow that the letter was not sent, for if despatched, it must have been handed to Washington in the camp at Cambridge, when the important concerns of the army rendered a record improbable, had any such record been deemed necessary. The tone and spirit of Boucher are genuine, and might be compared with many similar expressions struck off in the heat of party contest, and under the strong provocation of injuries inflicted by the "good people" of the Colonies upon real or suspected Tories. Social intercourse was interrupted, life long friendships broken off, and families divided by the political questions raised by the conduct of the British government towards America, and the intense bitterness engendered by these differences easily led to acts of persecution as cruel as they were unjust. The letter of Franklin to Strahan is merely another expression of the closing words of Boucher to Washington, and in the one case as in the other, relations were subsequently respected, when the results of the Revolution rendered a further nursing of injuries as foolish as it was unnecessary.

eight or nine years. You & I, alas! have not been the only Persons who have differed in our opinions; or who have found it impossible to agree. This is no Time nor Place for settling such Points; ere long, we shall all have to answer for them at a Tribunal, where alone it is of infinite moment that we should be justify'd.

How far you will agree with me in thinking it in your Power to do something for the Religious Interests of your Countrymen, I undertake not to say; but, I assure myself, we shall not differ by your thinking it of little, or no, moment. It cannot, I think, afford you Pleasure to reflect, how much has been done, through your means, for the Civil Concerns of your Country; & how little, as yet at least, for those of a higher Nature. That your Countrymen will be either better or happier by what has happened, permit me to say remains yet to be proved: I am sure, you wish they should; but it can be no Matter of Doubt or Dispute with any Man, that they can neither be so good nor so happy as they have been, if they are not religious. Many of the speculations which the late unsettled Times have given Birth to, resemble your Persimmons before the Frost: they are fair to the Eye and specious; but really disgusting & dangerous. This, in my mind, is the Case, in a particular manner, with many or most of the Utopian Projects, respecting Universal Equality, on the subject of Religious Establishments. I am unwilling to go deeply into the Investigation of this Question, though I want not Materials in Abundance, to show you, that it is romantic & mischievous in the extreme: because such a Discussion must needs be tiresome & tedious to you: suffice it, for the present, to remind you, that the Practice of the whole World is against you. Similar attempts, in similar Times. were made in these kingdoms: & if I were very anxious to set you against such Projects, I certainly could take no more effectual means, than by desiring you to remember what the Consequences of them were. In short, Sir, I hardly know a Point more capable of Demonstration—from History & Experience—than this is, that, to secure permanent national Felicity, some permanent national Religion is absolutely necessary.

I would hope in Virginia & Maryland at least, this would not be an unpopular opinion, as it certainly ought not: & I think certainly would not, if espoused & patronized by a Person that is popular. It is in this Light I view you; & this is the Reason of my having taken the Liberty to submit these suggestions to your consideration.

There are, at this time, in this country, candidates for Orders in the Church of England both from Virginia & Maryland: it will not surprise you, that, from the Changes that have taken Place, they should meet with Difficulties; nor does it surprize, though it greatly grieves me, that the Illwillers & Enemies of our Church, British as well as American, avail themselves of these unfortunate Circumstances, to discountenance & discourage our Church, if possible, still more than it is. Some of these Difficulties I hope, will be soon got over; & they all would, if the People of your States could think it right to shew a Desire only, that they might. It might, perhaps, as yet, be too much to ask for a Restoraⁿ of the old Establishment of the Church of England, though it be a measure which sound Policy will sooner or later adopt, & the longer it is delayed, the worse it will be: but, I hope it is not too much, nor too soon, to hope that, even now, the members of that church may be put on a Footing with Christians of other Denominations: which they never can be, till all the Ordinances of the Church are in their own Power, independent of any foreign

States : & among those Ordinances, that of ordination, &c., is most essential. In short, both Justice & Policy require that you should have a resident Bishop of your own, that your young Men may be ordained, as well as educated among yourselves.

I have no other interest in this measure, than what my Zeal for the Church & the best Interests of Mankind give me : but, believing as I do, that it is of great Moment, the Thing should be attended to, & soon, & that you are particularly concerned to attend to it, because no other Man can do it with such advantage. I could not be easy till I had thus satisfy'd my Conscience. Three years ago, I wrote you a Letter to the same Purpose ; but my Friends within the King's Lines, thinking that neither the Times nor yourself were then in a Temper to bear such applications, suppressed it. I have now done my Duty, & leave the Rest to Providence : & will add this only, that if, by any Means, either as I have studied the subject more than most Men, or as I happen to have Connexions in this Country, as well as yours, who are sincere & may be useful, Friends to such Measures, I beg leave to make you a Tender of my best services on the occasion.

It was, no Doubt, a great Mortification & Calamity to me to have all my American Property torn from me ; the Loss of my Character in that Country, which I little deserved, affected me much more, as you will allow it ought : but, I have lately felt the utmost Edge of keen sorrow, when it pleased Providence to deprive me of a true Friend, a most loving & beloved wife, for whom I was indebted to that Country. I pray God long to preserve you & yours from this the heaviest of all misfortunes.

With respectful Comp^{ts} to Mrs Washington,
I remain &c.

Dedication of Boucher's "View of the Causes and Consequences of the American Revolution."

To
GEORGE WASHINGTON ESQUIRE,
of Mount Vernon,
in Fairfax County, Virginia.

SIR,

In prefixing your name to a work avowedly hostile to that Revolution in which you bore a distinguished part, I am not conscious that I deserve to be charged with inconsistency. I do not address myself to the General of a Conventional Army ; but to the late dignified President of the United States, the friend of rational and sober freedom.

As a British subject I have observed with pleasure that the form of Government, under which you and your fellow-citizens now hope to find peace and happiness, however defective in many respects, has, in the unity of it's executive, and the division of it's legislative, powers, been framed after a British model. That, in the discharge of your duty as head of this Government, you have resisted those anarchical doctrines, which are hardly less dangerous to America than to Europe, is not more an eulogium, on the wisdom of our forefathers, than honourable to your individual wisdom and integrity.

As a Minister of Religion I am equally bound to tender you my respect for having (in your valedictory address to your countrymen) asserted your opinion that " the only firm supports of political prosperity are religion and morality;" and that "morality can be maintained only by religion." Those best friends of mankind, who, amidst all the din and uproar of Utopian reforms, persist to think that the affairs of this world can never be well administered by men trained to disregard the God who made it, must ever thank you for this decided protest against the fundamental maxim of modern revolutionists, that religion is no concern of the State.

It is on these grounds, Sir, that I now presume (and I hope not impertinently) to add my name to the list of those who have dedicated their works to you. One of them, not inconsiderable in fame, from having been your fulsome flatterer, has become your foul calumniator:* to such dedicators I am willing to persuade myself I have no resemblance. I bring no incense to your shrine even in a Dedication. Having never paid court to you whilst you shone in an exalted station, I am not so weak as to steer my little bark across the Atlantic in search of patronage and preferment; or so vain as to imagine that now, in the evening of my life, I may yet be warmed by your setting sun. My utmost ambition will be abundantly gratified by your condescending, as a private Gentleman in America, to receive with candour and kindness this disinterested testimony of regard from a private Clergyman in England. I was once your neighbour and your friend: the unhappy dispute, which terminated in the disunion of our respective countries, also broke off our personal connexion: but I never was more than your political enemy; and every sentiment even of political animosity has, on my part, long ago subsided. Permit me then to hope, that this tender of renewed amity between us may be received and regarded as giving some promise of that perfect reconciliation between our two countries which it is the sincere aim of this publication to promote. If, on this topic, there be another wish still nearer to my heart, it is that you would not think it beneath you to co-operate with so humble an effort to produce that reconciliation.

You have shewn great prudence (and, in my estimation, still greater patriotism) in resolving to terminate your days in retirement. To become, however, even at Mount Vernon, a mere private man, by divesting yourself of all public influence, is not in your power. I hope it is not your wish. Unincumbered with the distracting cares of public life, you may now, by the force of a still powerful example, gradually train the people around you to a love of order and subordination; and, above all, to a love of peace. "Hæ tibi erunt artes." That you possessed talents eminently well adapted for the high post you lately held, friends and foes have concurred in testifying: be it my pleasing task thus publicly to declare that you carry back to your paternal fields virtues equally calculated to bloom in the shade. To resemble Cincinnatus is but small praise: be it yours, Sir, to enjoy the calm repose and holy serenity of a Christian hero; and may "the Lord bless your latter end more than your beginning!"

I have the honour to be,
Sir,
Your very sincere Friend,
And most obedient humble Servant,

JONATHAN BOUCHER.

Epsom, Surrey, }
4th Nov. 1797. }

* Thomas Paine.

Washington to Boucher.

MOUNT VERNON, 15 August, 1798.

Revd Sir,

I know not how it is happened, but the fact is that your favor of the 8th of Novr last year is but just received, and at a time when both public and private business pressed so hard upon me, as to afford no leisure to give the " View of the Causes and Consequences of the American Revolution," written by you & which you had been pleased to send me, a perusal.

For the honor of its dedication, & for the friendly and favorable sentiments which are therein expressed, I pray you to accept my acknowledgment & thanks.

Not having read the Book, it follows of course that I can express no Opinion with respect to its political contents ; but I can venture to assert before hand & with confidence, that there is no man in either country more zealously devoted, to Peace and a good understanding between the two nations than I am, nor one who is more disposed to bury in oblivion all animosities which have subsisted between them & the individuals of each.

Peace with all the world, is my sincere wish. I am sure it is our true policy—and am persuaded it is the ardent desire of the Government. But there is a nation, whose intermeddling and restless disposition and attempts to divide, distract and influence the measures of other countries, that will not suffer us I fear to enjoy this blessing long, unless we will yield to them, our Rights and submit to greater injuries & insults than we have already sustained, to avoid the calamities resulting from War.

What will be the consequences of our arming for self defence, that Providence who permits these doings, in the disturbers of mankind & who rules and governs all things alone can tell. To its all powerful decrees we must submit. Whilst we hope that the justice of our cause, if war must ensue, will entitle us to its protections.

With very great Esteem, I am
Your most obed^t serv^t
G^o WASHINGTON